THE ULTIMATE

BOOK OF KNOWLEDGE

Derek O'Brien was born in Kolkata. He began his career as a journalist for *Sportsworld* magazine but soon shifted to advertising. After working for a number of very successful years as Creative Head of Ogilvy, Derek decided to focus all his energy and talent in his passion—quizzing.

Today, Derek is Asia's best-known quizmaster and the CEO of Derek O'Brien & Associates. He has been the host of the longest-running game show on Indian television, the Cadbury Bournvita Quiz Contest, for which he was voted the Best Anchor of a Game Show at the Indian Television Academy Awards for three years in a row. Always innovating, Derek is also credited with having conducted the first quiz on Twitter in 2010.

Derek has written over fifty bestselling reference, quiz and textbooks. In 2011, he was voted to the Rajya Sabha as a Member of Parliament (MP) and is the Leader of the Trinamool Congress Parliamentary Party in the Rajya Sabha and the chief national spokesperson.

Keep in touch with Derek on Twitter, where his handle is @quizderek, and on Facebook at www.facebook.com/MPDerekOBrien/

Other books by Derek O'Brien
(published by Rupa Publications)

Bournvita Quiz Contest Quiz Book 2012

The Ultimate BQC Book of Knowledge (Volumes 1 and 2)

The Best of BQC

Derek's Challenge

Speak Up, Speak Out: My Favourite Elocution Pieces and How to Deliver Them

My Way: Success Mantras of 12 Achievers

Derek Introduces: 100 Iconic Indians

Bournvita Quiz Contest Quiz Book 2014

BQC Quiz Book 3

The BQC Quiz Book 2017

THE ULTIMATE

BOOK OF KNOWLEDGE

DEREK O'BRIEN

Published by
Rupa Publications India Pvt. Ltd 2017
7/16, Ansari Road, Daryaganj
New Delhi 110002

Sales Centres:
Allahabad Bengaluru Chennai
Hyderabad Jaipur Kathmandu
Kolkata Mumbai

Copyright © Derek O'Brien & Associates 2017

'Cadbury' and 'Bournvita' are registered trademarks of
Cadbury India Limited.

All rights reserved.
No part of this publication may be reproduced, stored in a
retrieval system, or transmitted, in any form or by any means,
electronic, mechanical, photocopying, recording or otherwise,
without the prior permission of the publishers.

ISBN: 978-81-291-2991-8

First impression 2017

10 9 8 7 6 5 4 3 2 1

The moral right of the author has been asserted.

Printed and bound in India by Repro Knowledgecast Limited, Thane

This book is sold subject to the condition that it shall not,
by way of trade or otherwise, be lent, resold, hired out, or otherwise
circulated, without the publisher's prior consent, in any form of
binding or cover other than that in which it is published.

CONTENTS

Hall of Fame   *vii*

Art and Culture	1
Books and Comics	6
Entertainment	11
Food-I	16
Fun Facts-1	21
Food-II	23
General-I	28
Maths-1	33
General-II	34
Fun Facts-2	39
General-III	41
Geography	46
Maths-II	51
History-I	52
Fun Facts-3	57
History-II	59
Human Body	64
Maths-III	69
Nature And Wildlife	70
Politics	75

Fun Facts-4	81
Science and Technology	83
Sports-I	88
Maths-IV	93
Sports-II	94
Travel	99
Buzzer Round	104
Answers	121

HALL OF FAME

PAST WINNERS OF THE BOURNVITA QUIZ CONTEST

1994-1995, Mumbai

Campion High School, Mumbai
Balakrishnan Sivaraman, Sudhanshu Bhuwalka

1995-1996, Mumbai

Kendriya Vidyalaya, Powai, Mumbai
Eipy Koshy, Gourav Shah

1996-1997, Mumbai

Bombay International High School, Mumbai
Nirica Borges, Advait Behara

1997, Mumbai

Mount Saint Mary's School, New Delhi
Joe Christy, Maninder Singh Jessel

1997-1998, Mumbai

Bombay Scottish High School, Mumbai
Shaambhavi Pandyaa, Rahul Lalmalani

1998, Mumbai

Sacred Heart Convent School, Jamshedpur
Ela Verma, Lavanya Raghavan

1998-1999, Mumbai
Indian School Al Ghubra, Muscat
Anand Raghavan, Hitesh Kanvatirtha

1999, Mumbai
Maneckji Cooper High School, Mumbai
Ipsita Bandopadhyay, Gourav Bhattacharya

1999-2000, Mumbai
Chettinad Vidyashram, Chennai
Siddharth, Karthik Das

2000-2001, Mumbai
Bharatiya Vidya Bhavan, Hyderabad
Ananya Bhaskar, Aksha Anand

2001 September, Mumbai
Brightlands, Dehradun
Ankur Bharadwaj, Shray Sharma

2001 December, Mumbai
Little Flower High School, Hyderabad
G. Mithilesh, K Siddharth Reddy

2002 February, Bentota, Sri Lanka
G.D. Birla Centre For Education, Kolkata
Namrata Basu, Rituparna Dey

2002 June, Mumbai
Kerala Samajam Public School, Jamshedpur
Saurav Biswas, Kunal Mohan

2002 September, Mumbai
Jamnabai Narsee School, Mumbai
Sharan Narayanan, Vishnu Shrest

2003 January, Kerala
Naval Public High School, Mumbai
Apoorva Sharma, Abhishek Pandit

2003 May, Kolkata
St. Patrick's Higher Secondary School, Asansol
Pushpen Dasgupta, Shamik Ray

2003 October, Sangla
St. Agnes Loreto Day School, Lucknow
Aastha Srivastava, Illa Gupta

2004 February, Swabhumi, Kolkata
Apeejay School, Jalandhar
Mohit Thukral, Sahil Sareen

2004 May, Goa
Springdales School, Delhi
Anirudh Sridhar, B. Anuraag

2004 July, Indian Military Academy, Dehradun
The Mother's International School, Delhi
Krittika Adhikary, Milind Ganjoo

2004 November, Kolkata
Amity International, New Delhi
Aishwarya Singhal, Adarsh Modi

2005 August, Kolkata
Amity International, New Delhi
Utkarsh Johari, Aishwarya Singhal

2006 July, Kolkata
Riverdale High School, Dehradun
Kartikeya Panwar, Sumit Nair

2006 November, Kolkata
Seth Jaipuria School, Lucknow
Ratnaksha Lele, Ananya Kumar Singh

2011 August, Kolkata
Amity International School, Noida
Kripi Badonia, Shinjini Biswas

2012 January, Kolkata
Birla Vidya Niketan, New Delhi
Anusha Malhotra, Nitya Bansal

2013 January, Kolkata
Vidyaniketan Public School (Ullal), Bengaluru
Shashank Niranjan Gowda, Mainak Mandal

2014 December, Kolkata
Centre Point, Amravati Road, Nagpur
Ratnasambhav Sahu, Tanaya Ramani

2016 January, Shantiniketan
Brightlands, Dehradun
Arhaan Ahmad, Vishwas Chawla

ART AND CULTURE

1. Shata-tantri veena or the veena with a hundred strings was the original name of which musical instrument?
   a) Mridangam
   b) Santoor
   c) Jal Tarang
   d) Sitar
2. If you were attending the Natyanjali Dance Festival in Chidambaram, which state would you be in?
   a) Kerala
   b) Andhra Pradesh
   c) Tamil Nadu
   d) Uttar Pradesh
3. Which famous musician is believed to have invented the tabla?
   a) Tansen
   b) Mirza Ghalib
   c) Amir Khusrau
   d) Faiz Ahmed Faiz
4. On hearing about whose death did Ravi Shankar compose *Farewell, My Friend*?
   a) Mahatma Gandhi
   b) Lady Diana
   c) Satyajit Ray
   d) John F. Kennedy
5. Who said this after winning a Grammy: 'I've been appreciated only twice by my guru, Ustad Allah Rakha'?

a) Amjad Ali Khan
   b) Bismillah Khan
   c) Zakir Hussain
   d) Rashid Khan
6. In 2010, M.F. Husain was conferred the nationality of...
   a) Qatar
   b) Oman
   c) Germany
   d) South Africa
7. Whom did Nand Das base his initial plays of the Rasleela on?
   a) Rama
   b) Krishna
   c) Hanuman
   d) Arjuna
8. Which musical instrument is known as klavier in German?
   a) Piano
   b) Trumpet
   c) Mouth organ
   d) Guitar
9. Which of these theatre forms originated in Kerala?
   a) Nautanki
   b) Koodiyattam
   c) Bhavai
   d) Bhaona
10. The name of which percussion instrument literally means 'body of clay'?
    a) Mridangam
    b) Sitar
    c) Tabla

d) Ektara
11. In the arts, what do Rishabh, Gandhar and Nishad have in common?
    a) Types of dances
    b) Styles of painting
    c) Notes of classical music
    d) Types of kebabs
12. In Madhya Pradesh, which field is awarded the Tansen Samman?
    a) Classical music
    b) Literature
    c) Sports
    d) Physics
13. Name the illustrious son of Padma Bhushan recipient Haafiz Ali Khan.
    a) Amjad Ali Khan
    b) Hariprasad Chaurasia
    c) Shiv Kumar Sharma
    d) Zakir Hussain
14. In Indian classical music, which note comes just before 're'?
    a) Pa
    b) Ga
    c) So
    d) Sa
15. Who composed a number of songs and plays under the pen name Akhtari Pia?
    a) Munshi Premchand
    b) Nawab Wajid Ali Shah
    c) Tansen
    d) Akbar

16. In Kathakali, which of these represents noble or good characters?
    a) Green make-up
    b) No make-up
    c) Blue make-up
    d) Black make-up
17. Which animal became a central part of M.F. Husain's paintings from the 1950s?
    a) Horse
    b) Lion
    c) Dragon
    d) Rat
18. In Indian music, what is the term given to the first line of a song or composition?
    a) Mukhda
    b) Sargam
    c) Taal
    d) Antara
19. In which dance form is the dancer usually dressed in a white and gold-bordered Kasavu saree?
    a) Odissi
    b) Kathak
    c) Mohiniattam
    d) Bharatanatyam
20. Which musician of India is the book *Abba...God's Greatest Gift to Us* based on?
    a) Bismillah Khan
    b) Amjad Ali Khan
    c) Rashid Khan
    d) Bade Ghulam Ali Khan

21. Who is the only Indian musician in Mick Jagger's music group Superheavy?
    a) Zakir Hussain
    b) Karan Johar
    c) A.R. Rahman
    d) Salman Khan
22. What are Bhairavi, Asavari and Todi different types of?
    a) Martial art forms
    b) Rivers
    c) Sarods
    d) Ragas
23. What is known as kolam in Tamil Nadu, mandana in Rajasthan and aripana in Bihar?
    a) Sitar
    b) Carpet
    c) Rangoli
    d) Chikan embroidery
24. Which of these is generally held with one hand and played with the other?
    a) Tabla
    b) Xylophone
    c) Mridangam
    d) Duffli
25. Which of these states would you associate patola weaving with?
    a) Gujarat
    b) West Bengal
    c) Jammu and Kashmir
    d) Nagaland

BOOKS AND COMICS

1. Who published his first poems at the age of sixteen under the pseudonym Bhanushingho, meaning 'the Sun Lion'?
   a) Pranab Mukherjee
   b) Rabindranath Tagore
   c) Bankim Chandra Chatterjee
   d) Kazi Nazrul Islam
2. I am a lazy fat cat who hates Mondays, loves lasagna, and my owner is Jon Arbuckle. Which cartoon character am I?
   a) Crookshanks
   b) Garfield
   c) Tom
   d) Cheshire Cat
3. Whose name is used to describe a moneylender charging high rates of interest?
   a) Hamlet
   b) Shylock
   c) Romeo
   d) Lady Macbeth
4. In which language did R.K. Narayan write most of his works?
   a) Hindi
   b) English
   c) Kannada
   d) Punjabi

5. Which of these characters was not created by Agatha Christie?
   a) Thomas Beresford
   b) Perry Mason
   c) Parker Pyne
   d) Hercule Poirot
6. *Man of Everest*, also published as *Tiger of the Snows*, is the autobiography of…
   a) Tenzing Norgay
   b) Edmund Hillary
   c) George Mallory
   d) Reinhold Messner
7. Name the pet tiger of the cartoon character Calvin.
   a) Hobbes
   b) Ruff
   c) Hot Dog
   d) Snoopy
8. In the language of the apes, whose name means 'white skin'?
   a) Mowgli
   b) Peter Pan
   c) Tarzan
   d) Goldilocks
9. What was the name of Robinson Crusoe's servant?
   a) Monday
   b) Wednesday
   c) Friday
   d) Saturday
10. Which of these works was first published in a children's magazine as The Sea-Cook?
    a) *Alice's Adventures in Wonderland*

b) *Treasure Island*
c) *The Adventures of Huckleberry Finn*
d) *Gulliver's Travels*

11. The island Más a Tierra on which Alexander Selkirk was marooned, has now officially changed its name to what?
    a) Robinson Crusoe Island
    b) Treasure Island
    c) Captain Nemo Island
    d) Gulliver Island

12. Of all these characters created by William Shakespeare, who has the most lines to deliver?
    a) Lady Macbeth
    b) Hamlet
    c) Othello
    d) Romeo

13. The television series Bharat Ek Khoj was based on a book written by whom?
    a) Jawaharlal Nehru
    b) C. Rajagopalachari
    c) Dr Rajendra Prasad
    d) Subhas Chandra Bose

14. Which Indian literary work has been retold by Kamban in Tamil, Madhava Kandali in Assamese and Krittibas Ojha in Bengali?
    a) Mahabharata
    b) Ramayana
    c) Jataka Tales
    d) Meghaduta

15. Who is the CEO of Wayne Enterprises?
    a) Spider-Man

b) Batman
c) Captain America
d) Superman

16. Which work by Shakespeare is considered unlucky as it is believed that the lines contain magic spells?
    a) *Macbeth*
    b) *Hamlet*
    c) *The Merchant of Venice*
    d) *David Copperfield*

17. Which is the official and most widely spoken language of Brazil?
    a) Italian
    b) Portuguese
    c) Arabic
    d) German

18. Which novel is based on the life of William Dampier, who sailed around the globe three times?
    a) *Gulliver's Travels*
    b) *Around the World in 80 Days*
    c) *The Three Musketeers*
    d) *Black Beauty*

19. The Tunnel of Time is the autobiography of which author and cartoonist?
    a) R.K. Laxman
    b) Mario Miranda
    c) Abu Abraham
    d) Satyajit Ray

20. In the Hindi translation of *Tintin*, what is the dog Snowy's name?
    a) Tommy
    b) Natkhat

c) Chulbul
   d) Shwet
21. According to UNESCO, which Indian work is the oldest text available in the world?
   a) Rig Veda
   b) Devdas
   c) Guru Granth Sahib
   d) The Constitution of India
22. On his last voyage, who was asked to collect the tusks of five hundred elephants?
   a) Gulliver
   b) Sindbad
   c) Aladdin
   d) Phileas Fogg
23. In *Ali Baba and the Forty Thieves*, what was Ali Baba's profession?
   a) Milkman
   b) Woodcutter
   c) Goldsmith
   d) Cobbler
24. Which famous person's life forms the central plot of the novel Queen of Glory?
   a) Shahnaz Husain
   b) Rani Lakshmi Bai
   c) Gayatri Devi
   d) Mother Teresa
25. The book Singhasan Battisi is the story of which king?
   a) Vikramaditya
   b) Shivaji
   c) King Lear
   d) Akbar

ENTERTAINMENT

1. Which one of these was Salman Khan and Katrina Kaif's first film together?
   a) *Maine Pyar Kyun Kiya*
   b) *Ek Tha Tiger*
   c) *Rajneeti*
   d) *Race*
2. What kind of animal was Richard Parker in the film Life of Pi?
   a) Lion
   b) Tiger
   c) Horse
   d) Camel
3. In which film do cricketers Andrew Symonds, Herschelle Gibbs and Nasser Hussain appear together?
   a) *Mother India*
   b) *Band Baaja Baaraat*
   c) *3 Idiots*
   d) *Patiala House*
4. *The Last Lear* was the first English language film of which actor?
   a) Amitabh Bachchan
   b) Irrfan Khan
   c) Naseeruddin Shah
   d) Om Puri
5. Who played the role of Haider in the 2014 film of the same name?

a) Varun Dhawan
   b) Shahid Kapoor
   c) Akshay Kumar
   d) Ranbir Kapoor
6. Which film connects Meena Kumari, Moushumi Chatterjee and Vidya Balan?
   a) *Devdas*
   b) *Balika Vadhu*
   c) *Dil Chahta Hai*
   d) *Parineeta*
7. The name of which Akshay Kumar film was taken from a tagline behind a truck?
   a) *Khiladi*
   b) *Singh is Kinng*
   c) *Dabangg*
   d) *Khatta Meetha*
8. In the film *Jodhaa Akbar*, if Hrithik Roshan was Akbar, who played the role of Jodha?
   a) Rani Mukherjee
   b) Aishwarya Rai
   c) Katrina Kaif
   d) Deepika Padukone
9. Who was the music director of the 2014 film *Highway*?
   a) Vishal Dadlani
   b) Himesh Reshammiya
   c) Pritam
   d) A.R. Rahman
10. Who sang his first song for the Assamese film *Indramalati*, at the age of twelve?
    a) S D Burman
    b) Jagjit Singh

c) Kishore Kumar
   d) Bhupen Hazarika
11. *Rockstar* was the last released film of which legendary actor?
    a) Raj Kapoor
    b) Shammi Kapoor
    c) Sunil Dutt
    d) Dev Anand
12. For which film did Karan Johar win the Filmfare Best Director Award in 2011?
    a) *Kuch Kuch Hota Hai*
    b) *My Name is Khan*
    c) *Kal Ho Na Ho*
    d) *Taare Zameen Par*
13. According to Google, which was the most searched Indian film in 2012?
    a) *Jannat 2*
    b) *Kahaani*
    c) *Ek Tha Tiger*
    d) *Agent Vinod*
14. Who played the role of the young Sunny Deol in the 1983 film *Betaab*?
    a) Sonu Nigam
    b) Virat Kohli
    c) Hrithik Roshan
    d) Ranbir Kapoor
15. Which actor was only six years old when he appeared in his first film *Aasha*?
    a) Saif Ali Khan
    b) Salman Khan
    c) Hrithik Roshan
    d) Aamir Khan

16. Rajiv Hari Om Bhatia was a martial arts instructor before he changed his profession. Who is he better known as today?
    a) Akshay Kumar
    b) Baba Ramdev
    c) Sunny Deol
    d) Vijender Singh
17. Who was the director of the 2013 film *Vishwaroopam*?
    a) Prakash Raj
    b) Rohit Shetty
    c) Rajnikanth
    d) Kamal Haasan
18. Abdul Rashid Salim are part of which actor's full name?
    a) Aamir Khan
    b) Shah Rukh Khan
    c) Irrfan Khan
    d) Salman Khan
19. Which of these actresses is a former Miss World?
    a) Anushka Sharma
    b) Aishwarya Rai
    c) Sushmita Sen
    d) Katrina Kaif
20. Who returned to the silver screen after fourteen years with the film *English Vinglish*?
    a) Karisma Kapoor
    b) Sridevi
    c) Juhi Chawla
    d) Madhuri Dixit
21. Shah Rukh Khan has played the role of which emperor of the Mauryan dynasty?

a) Bindusara
b) Ashoka
c) Chandragupta Maurya
d) Dev Burman

22. Which of these actresses made her debut in a film with Salman Khan?
    a) Anushka Sharma
    b) Deepika Padukone
    c) Nargis
    d) Sonakshi Sinha

23. Who received the Filmfare Lifetime Achievement Award in 1991?
    a) Dilip Kumar
    b) Amitabh Bachchan
    c) Rajesh Khanna
    d) Lata Mangeshkar

24. In a textbook, the chapter titled From Bus Conductor To Superstar, is based on whose life?
    a) M.G. Ramachandran
    b) Rajinikanth
    c) M.S. Swaminathan
    d) Gundappa Viswanath

25. Who is the director of the 2011 film *Don 2*?
    a) Steven Spielberg
    b) Farhan Akhtar
    c) Karan Johar
    d) Gauri Khan

FOOD-I

1. The name of which fruit comes from the Latin words for 'seeded apple'?
   a) Litchi
   b) Banana
   c) Orange
   d) Pomegranate
2. Which of these food items is said to have been created by Ashok Vaidya in Mumbai?
   a) Lal maans
   b) Mysore pak
   c) Petha
   d) Vada pav
3. Kanthari, Kashmiri, Jwala and Dhaani are varieties of which spice in India?
   a) Chilli
   b) Vanilla
   c) Cardamom
   d) Ginger
4. Which country is known for Cantonese and Szechwan cooking styles?
   a) Japan
   b) China
   c) Italy
   d) Portugal
5. What comes in two basic shapes: snowflake and mushroom?
   a) Pasta

b) Cake
   c) Ice cream
   d) Popped popcorn
6. If a Britisher calls it an aubergine, what do we usually call it?
   a) Cauliflower
   b) Potato
   c) Brinjal
   d) Cabbage
7. What was known by names such as 'gola' and 'satha' in the eighteenth century?
   a) Onion
   b) Potato
   c) Cauliflower
   d) Radish
8. Which of these is generally eaten with 'makke di roti'?
   a) Bhatura
   b) Pizza
   c) Biryani
   d) Sarson da saag
9. Which of these is sometimes called 'vilaayati baingan'?
   a) Tomato
   b) Onion
   c) Lady's finger
   d) Bittergourd
10. An imarti resembles which of these?
    a) Barfi
    b) Idli
    c) Jalebi
    d) Samosa

11. Which of these is also known as golgappa, phuchka or gup chup?
    a) Panipuri
    b) Samosa
    c) Lassi
    d) Sohan halwa
12. What is the most commonly eaten part of a carrot plant?
    a) Root
    b) Leaf
    c) Branch
    d) Flower
13. Which state is the largest producer of apples in India?
    a) Rajasthan
    b) Jammu and Kashmir
    c) Jharkhand
    d) Tamil Nadu
14. Which of these words comes from the Arabic word meaning 'that which prevents sleep'?
    a) Coffee
    b) Tea
    c) Ice cream
    d) Chocolate
15. Citrus reticulata is the most important commercial species of which fruit in India?
    a) Apple
    b) Mango
    c) Banana
    d) Orange
16. In 2011, this was named as the world's most popular dish in a global survey conducted by the charity

Oxfam. Which one is it?
a) Sandwich
b) Biscuit
c) Pasta
d) Pizza

17. What is the main ingredient of the dish rogan josh?
a) Egg
b) Meat
c) Paneer
d) Mushroom

18. Which of these vegetables bears the scientific name Solanum tuberosum?
a) Carrot
b) Tomato
c) Potato
d) Brinjal

19. Which spice is also known as yellow ginger?
a) Saunf
b) Turmeric
c) Cardamom
d) Jalebi

20. The name of which of these sweets comes from a Persian word meaning 'icy or snowy'?
a) Laddoo
b) Barfi
c) Jalebi
d) Rasgulla

21. Who is regarded as the 'Father of the White Revolution' in India?
a) Sundarlal Bahuguna
b) Baba Amte

c) V. Kurien
d) M.S. Swaminathan

22. Which country is the world's largest producer of coffee?
    a) Brazil
    b) USA
    c) Cuba
    d) India

23. During World War II, which of these was used when intravenous (IV) solution was in short supply?
    a) Coconut water
    b) Rainwater
    c) Tea
    d) Orange juice

24. In which state does the 'Vasta Waza' supervise a special thirty-six course meal known as 'Wazwan'?
    a) Jammu and Kashmir
    b) Uttar Pradesh
    c) Tamil Nadu
    d) Karnataka

25. Traditionally, which of these sweets is soaked in milk?
    a) Jalebi
    b) Rasgulla
    c) Lollipop
    d) Rasmalai

FUN FACTS-1

1. Few people knew about Nek Chand's rock garden in Chandigarh while he was working on it. He secretly worked on it in his spare time for many years.
2. Madhubani painting was traditionally done only by the women of the Mithila region of Bihar. Today, it is also done by the men of the area in order to meet the growing demand for these paintings.
3. The first self-adhesive stamps were issued by Sierra Leone in early 1964.
4. Animal Farm: A Fairy Story, A Satire, or A Contemporary Satire was the original title of George Orwell's *Animal Farm*.
5. Because of its location in the centre of South America, Paraguay is sometimes called the 'Heart of America'.
6. Dalmatians get their name from Dalmatia, a region lying mostly within present-day Croatia.
7. The liver can regenerate if a part of it is removed due to injury or disease.
8. A file cabinet labelled 0–Z is said to have inspired L. Frank Baum to call his famous fictional kingdom 'OZ'.
9. Istanbul, the largest city in Turkey, is located on a peninsula between Europe and Asia.
10. The pink colour of the flamingo comes from the algae and shrimp it eats.
11. The word 'volcano' comes from the name of the

Roman God of Fire, Vulcan.
12. The Queen of the Andes plant blooms only once every eighty or more years.
13. According to legend, after Udai Singh lost Chittorgarh, he was told by a holy man to establish his capital on the hill near Lake Pichola. Maharana Udai Singh founded Udaipur in the area recommended by the holy man.
14. The only Indians to bat on all five days of a Test are M.L. Jaisimha and Ravi Shastri.
15. The first website in the world, http://info.cern.ch, was launched on 6 August 1991.

FOOD-II

1. Which of these is a ball of deep-fried paneer boiled in sugar syrup?
   a) Gajar halwa
   b) Gulab jamun
   c) Shrikhand
   d) Kulfi
2. Which fruit has varieties like Allahabad Safeda, Banarasi, Chittidar and Harijha?
   a) Apple
   b) Banana
   c) Orange
   d) Guava
3. In 1877, what was first produced in Bikaner during the reign of Maharaja Dungar Singh?
   a) Rasgulla
   b) Bhujia
   c) Idli
   d) Thekua
4. Which of these fruits is also known as Indian gooseberry?
   a) Angoor
   b) Amrood
   c) Amla
   d) Anar
5. Which spice, known as zanjabil in Arabic, is the dried underground stem of a herbaceous tropical plant?
   a) Garlic

b) Ginger
   c) Chilli
   d) Coriander
6. Trinidad Scorpion Butch T, Bhut Jolokia and Naga Viper are varieties of which of the following?
   a) Scorpions
   b) Chillies
   c) Stamps
   d) Tea
7. Which of these is a popular Tibetan noodle soup?
   a) Dhokla
   b) Upma
   c) Idli
   d) Thukpa
8. Which of these is usually sold in square or diamond shapes?
   a) Gulab jamun
   b) Motichoor laddoo
   c) Barfi
   d) Jalebi
9. Which of these is another name for lady's finger?
   a) Okra
   b) Methi
   c) Kaddu
   d) Saunf
10. Which of these is normally produced by freezing in small containers?
    a) Rasgulla
    b) Kulfi
    c) Jalebi
    d) Petha

11. Which word is common to the cooking of an egg and an illegal action?
    a) Boil
    b) Skillet
    c) Poach
    d) Scramble
12. In the poem 'Johnny Johnny...', what was Johnny eating?
    a) Sugar
    b) Chocolate
    c) Apple
    d) Orange
13. Which of these sweets is also the name of a film directed by Anurag Basu?
    a) Rasgulla
    b) Laddoo
    c) Barfi
    d) Sandesh
14. Which spice is called zafran in Arabic?
    a) Saffron
    b) Turmeric
    c) Ginger
    d) Garlic
15. Which of these is served as sliced meat roasted on a spit?
    a) Falafel
    b) Shawarma
    c) Hummus
    d) Keema
16. Raisins are partially dried forms of which of these?
    a) Oranges

b) Dates
c) Grapes
d) Cherries

17. Which of these food items shares its name with a famous lane in Delhi?
    a) Paratha
    b) Tandoori
    c) Paneer
    d) Rezala

18. The famous layered dessert 'bebinca', made of flour, coconut milk and eggs in a clay oven, is a speciality of this state in India. Name the state.
    a) Goa
    b) Karnataka
    c) Nagaland
    d) Punjab

19. What is the colour of the circle on the symbol for vegetarian food, found on food packets?
    a) Brown
    b) White
    c) Green
    d) Blue

20. Which of these varieties of mangoes is named after a Portuguese general?
    a) Alphonso
    b) Banganapalli
    c) Fazli
    d) Chausa

21. What is the most common method of potato preparation across the world?
    a) Boiling

b) Deep frying
   c) Pickling
   d) Mashing
22. What is Chhota Bheem's favourite sweet?
   a) Laddoo
   b) Barfi
   c) Jalebi
   d) Rasgulla
23. Which spice is called 'cilantro' in Spanish?
   a) Coriander
   b) Cardamom
   c) Clove
   d) Pepper
24. Which food item was used before erasers to erase pencil marks?
   a) Bread crumbs
   b) Salt
   c) Wheat dough
   d) Rice
25. The Aztecs gave it a name meaning 'bitter water', and they added vanilla and chillies to it for flavour. What is it?
   a) Coffee
   b) Chocolate
   c) Tea
   d) Potato

GENERAL-I

1. In which part of the human body is a paranda worn?
   a) Hair
   b) Wrist
   c) Neck
   d) Elbow
2. On whose life is the documentary Yes Madam, Sir based?
   a) Indira Gandhi
   b) Kiran Bedi
   c) Sushma Swaraj
   d) Priyanka Chopra
3. In 1863, cartoonist Thomas Nast was the first to paint whose definitive portrait?
   a) Santa Claus
   b) Shivaji
   c) Queen Victoria
   d) Mickey Mouse
4. Bharat Ratna, 1990; Nobel Peace Prize, 1993; Gandhi Peace Prize, 2000—who are we referring to?
   a) Dalai Lama
   b) Nelson Mandela
   c) Mother Teresa
   d) Aung San Suu Kyi
5. According to reports published in 2007, over 20 per cent of the decorative gold used throughout the world was used in...
   a) Indian sarees

b) Minting coins
c) Pasta
d) Tooth fillings
6. Which word is common to a punctuation mark, the large intestine and the currency of Costa Rica?
   a) Asterisk
   b) Colon
   c) Apostrophe
   d) Full stop
7. How many zeros would you write after one, if you had to write one crore in numerals?
   a) Two
   b) Five
   c) Six
   d) Seven
8. How many US presidents have been awarded the Nobel Peace Prize?
   a) Two
   b) Three
   c) Four
   d) Five
9. If you were writing in English, the capital of which of these would have the longest name?
   a) Andhra Pradesh
   b) Maharashtra
   c) Lakshadweep
   d) Gujarat
10. In Assam, on which part of the body would you wear a jaapi made from bamboo?
    a) Head
    b) Nose

c) Ankle
   d) Waist
11. The shades of which of these is measured by the Fischer-Saller scale?
   a) Hair colour
   b) Eye colour
   c) Nail colour
   d) Colour of the tongue
12. Which Nobel Prize has never been shared by three laureates?
   a) Peace
   b) Literature
   c) Economics
   d) Chemistry
13. In 1920, the League of Nations internationally standardized the format of...
   a) Driving licences
   b) Shoes
   c) Traffic signals
   d) Passports
14. The flag of which of these countries is different on the front and back?
   a) Paraguay
   b) Switzerland
   c) Nepal
   d) Libya
15. Mohair is the yarn made from which animal's hair?
   a) Goat
   b) Rabbit
   c) Elephant
   d) Yak

16. Who was the last non-Indian to have been awarded the Bharat Ratna?
    a) Winston Churchill
    b) George Washington
    c) Khan Abdul Gaffar Khan
    d) Nelson Mandela
17. In 1973, which country produced stamps in the shape of records that could be played?
    a) Japan
    b) Pakistan
    c) Bhutan
    d) India
18. According to the NATO phonetic alphabet, 'I' is the code for which country?
    a) Indonesia
    b) Iran
    c) India
    d) Islamabad
19. The Roman Acta Diurna, appearing in 59 BCE, was the earliest recorded form of a...
    a) Birth certificate
    b) Quiz book
    c) Calendar
    d) Newspaper
20. Traditionally, chikankari was done on white cloth with threads of this colour. Name the colour.
    a) White
    b) Red
    c) Orange
    d) Green

21. In which category did Mother Teresa win the Nobel Prize?
    a) Peace
    b) Physics
    c) Medicine
    d) Economics
22. After China and India, which is the third most populous country in the world?
    a) Brazil
    b) USA
    c) Russia
    d) Vatican City
23. What are you most likely to buy using the D-Z Colour Grading Scale?
    a) Mango
    b) Diamond
    c) Silk
    d) Nail polish
24. If crude oil is the most traded commodity in the world, which is the second?
    a) Coffee
    b) Bamboo
    c) Roses
    d) Brinjal
25. Which of these is a knee-length coat buttoning to the neck, worn by men from South Asia?
    a) Sherwani
    b) Mekhala
    c) Poncho
    d) Capri

MATHS-1

Please go sequentially from left to right (not following BODMAS)

You can use addition, subtraction, multiplication or division to figure out the correct answer:

1.	30		6		4		8	=	1
2.	20		30		4		25	=	8
3.	41		15		17		13	=	3
4.	60		24		5		10	=	18
5.	45		3		10		2	=	50
6.	55		34		7		11	=	33
7.	25		6		55		19	=	5
8.	67		3		47		11	=	14

GENERAL-II

1. Abul Asar Hafeez Jullundhri wrote the national anthem of which country?
   a) Bangladesh
   b) Nepal
   c) Indonesia
   d) Pakistan
2. The Bronze Wolf is the only award given by which organization?
   a) World Scout Committee
   b) Lions Clubs International
   c) Red Cross
   d) Filmfare Awards Committee
3. Which international award is given out every year on December 10?
   a) Nobel Prize
   b) Arjuna Award
   c) Oscars
   d) Filmfare Awards
4. The value and durability of the Kashmiri carpet depends on the…
   a) Amount of thread used
   b) Knots per square inch
   c) Number of colours used
   d) Amount of snowfall
5. In which part of the human body is a jhanjhar worn?
   a) Neck
   b) Ear

c) Wrist
   d) Ankle
6. Who were the first people to use paper money?
   a) Chinese
   b) Greeks
   c) Mexicans
   d) Egyptians
7. What is the maximum number of people allowed to share a Nobel Prize?
   a) Two
   b) Three
   c) Four
   d) Thirteen
8. In Venice, a gondola is a type of...
   a) Boat
   b) Stringed instrument
   c) Sweet
   d) Paper
9. Bond, bristol and kraft are varieties of which article?
   a) Combs
   b) Handkerchiefs
   c) Paper
   d) Shoes
10. If jodhpurs are trousers for horse riding, what are patialas?
    a) Tea cups
    b) Pleated salwars
    c) Embroidered bags
    d) Painted carpets
11. In 1996, who became the fourth honorary citizen of the United States?

    a) Mahatma Gandhi
    b) Mother Teresa
    c) Satyajit Ray
    d) Zakir Hussain
12. In 800 CE, Lu Yu wrote the first book on...
    a) Silk
    b) Tea
    c) Kangaroos
    d) Quizzing
13. According to the US Census Bureau, which country will be the most populous nation by the year 2025?
    a) India
    b) USA
    c) Japan
    d) Australia
14. Which of these is an eye cosmetic?
    a) Surma
    b) Gajra
    c) Bindi
    d) Kundal
15. On which part of the human body would you generally wear a beanie?
    a) Wrist
    b) Head
    c) Ankle
    d) Waist
16. The names of how many states of India end with the letter 'h'?
    a) One
    b) Five
    c) Six

d) Twelve
17. In Roman numerals, what does 'XL' stand for?
    a) 30
    b) 40
    c) 50
    d) 60
18. In most cars, which of these is controlled by the driver's foot?
    a) Indicator lights
    b) Wiper
    c) Clutch
    d) Gear
19. Which of the following is a textile dyeing technique native to the island of Java?
    a) Chikankari
    b) Batik
    c) Phulkari
    d) Ikat
20. Who among these developed a system of writing for the blind?
    a) Louis Braille
    b) Helen Keller
    c) Alexander Graham Bell
    d) James Cook
21. Accidentally invented by Thomas Sullivan, which of these has 2,000 perforations or small holes?
    a) Mosquito net
    b) Tea bag
    c) Postage stamp
    d) Beehive

22. How many zeros must you add to the number hundred to reach ten lakh?
    a) Four
    b) Five
    c) Eight
    d) Ten
23. The 2011 Nobel Peace Prize was shared by three women. Two were from Liberia. Which country was the third woman from?
    a) USA
    b) Yemen
    c) China
    d) Pakistan
24. Only two women have received the Bharat Ratna in music: Lata Mangeshkar and...
    a) Shreya Ghoshal
    b) Alka Yagnik
    c) Asha Bhosle
    d) M.S. Subbulakshmi
25. Who was the first non-Nepali to receive honorary citizenship of Nepal?
    a) Edmund Hillary
    b) Sonam Kapoor
    c) Neil Armstrong
    d) Abraham Lincoln

FUN FACTS-2

1. After becoming the ruler of Delhi, Razziya Sultan gave up wearing feminine clothes and discarded the veil. She started wearing the clothes and headdress worn by the men of the time.
2. In the late 1870s, cats were used to deliver mail in Liege, Belgium. The cats carried bundles of letters to villages within a 30 km radius of the city centre.
3. Tony Stark or Iron Man has two master's degrees in electrical engineering from the Massachusetts Institute of Technology.
4. The population of Asia is larger than the combined population of all other continents.
5. A person who studies spiders is called an arachnologist.
7. The covering at the end of a shoelace is called an aglet.
8. The letter e is the most frequently used letter in the English alphabet.
9. The tail of a peacock is more than half the total length of its body.
10. Thailand is famous for its tuk-tuks, three-wheeled vehicles with open sides and a covered top.
11. The Buland Darwaza was built to commemorate Akbar's victory in Gujarat.
12. The literacy rate in India has gone up from 64.83 per cent in 2001 to 74.04 per cent in 2011.
13. Kang, a popular sport of Manipur, is played only

during the period between Cheiraoba and the Rath Yatra festival. It is believed that evil spirits invade the minds of the players if the game is played beyond its specified time period.

14. Twitter did not want to call the posts on its site as 'tweets'. The company wanted to use 'status updates' instead, but gave in after users insisted on using 'tweets'.

15. It is said that the roads of Rome were sprinkled with saffron when Nero went into the city.

GENERAL-III

1. Phulkari, meaning 'flower work', is a form of which of these?
   a) Embroidery
   b) Sculpting
   c) Paper folding
   d) Flower arranging
2. Apart from green, which colour is common to the flags of Pakistan and India?
   a) White
   b) Saffron
   c) Navy blue
   d) Red
3. The writer Washington Irving was the first person to assert that Father Christmas or Santa Claus…
   a) Wears a red outfit
   b) Slides down chimneys
   c) Owns Rudolph the reindeer
   d) Lives in London
4. In an alphabetical list of state capitals of India, which state capital would come last?
   a) Maharashtra
   b) West Bengal
   c) Tamil Nadu
   d) Kerala
5. 'Sayaun Thunga Phool Ka' is the national anthem of which country?
   a) Bhutan

b) Nepal
c) Sri Lanka
d) Maldives

6. Spread, button-down, forward point and club are types of which of the following?
   a) Collars
   b) Skirts
   c) Shoes
   d) Sleeves

7. Which object on the new flag of Bhutan was first painted by Kilkhor Lopen Jada?
   a) Dragon
   b) Lion
   c) Maple leaf
   d) Star

8. How many thousand rupee notes would you need in India to become a crorepati?
   a) Hundred
   b) Thousand
   c) Ten thousand
   d) One lakh

9. Which mathematical sign was introduced by Robert Recorde in 1557?
   a) Equals to
   b) Plus
   c) Minus
   d) Percentage

10. The muslin handkerchief given by Nur Jehan to Jahangir is said to have popularized which of these?
    a) Zardozi
    b) Chikankari

c) Batik
   d) Applique
11. Which colour appears between blue and yellow in a rainbow?
    a) Red
    b) Green
    c) Orange
    d) Indigo
12. The tie and dye process is generally used in which of these sarees??
    a) Benarasi
    b) Paithani
    c) Bandhni
    d) Jamdani
13. Which colour is common to the flags of Albania and Algeria?
    a) Green
    b) Red
    c) Blue
    d) Yellow
14. Which of these is a long coat worn by men in India?
    a) Pheta
    b) Jodhpurs
    c) Garara
    d) Achkan
15. In India, which profession would you pursue with an LLB degree?
    a) Medicine
    b) Law
    c) Architecture
    d) Quizzing

16. Which famous person once said: 'By blood, I am Albanian. By citizenship, an Indian... As to my calling, I belong to the world...'?
    a) Nelson Mandela
    b) Jawaharlal Nehru
    c) Mother Teresa
    d) Mahatma Gandhi
17. Which of these items of clothing is not named after an island?
    a) Capris
    b) Bermudas
    c) Cargos
    d) Hawaiian shirts
18. In the 1940s, the map on this flag was redrawn by cartographer Leo Drozdoff. Which organization did the flag belong to?
    a) United Nations
    b) European Union
    c) Bhutan
    d) Sri Lanka
19. Which neighbouring country's currency is known as kyat?
    a) Myanmar
    b) Sri Lanka
    c) Bangladesh
    d) Pakistan
20. Which princely state's currency was designated as the Osmania sicca?
    a) Hyderabad
    b) Patiala
    c) Gwalior

d) Bhopal
21. Platform, Pointe, Oxford and Mary Jane are different types of…
    a) Shoes
    b) Bags
    c) Bracelets
    d) Trousers
22. The word 'pashmina' comes from the Persian word for…
    a) Silk
    b) Cotton
    c) Wool
    d) Jute
23. The rupee is the currency of which of these countries?
    a) Bhutan
    b) Myanmar
    c) Afghanistan
    d) Mauritius
24. In 2014, India regained its position as the largest consumer of gold in the world from which country?
    a) China
    b) USA
    c) Italy
    d) Germany
25. Which of the following is not a natural fibre?
    a) Silk
    b) Cotton
    c) Nylon
    d) Jute

GEOGRAPHY

1. Which is the tallest free-standing mountain in the world?
   a) Everest
   b) Kilimanjaro
   c) Fuji
   d) Kanchenjunga
2. Which of these cities is built on Salsette Island?
   a) Islamabad
   b) New Delhi
   c) Chandigarh
   d) Mumbai
3. Which of these states of India has only two districts?
   a) West Bengal
   b) Sikkim
   c) Goa
   d) Uttar Pradesh
4. Which of these is the source of 20 per cent of all free-flowing fresh water on Earth?
   a) Dead Sea
   b) Mt. Everest
   c) Niagara Falls
   d) Amazon Rainforest
5. Which of these is a landlocked state?
   a) Kerala
   b) Gujarat
   c) West Bengal
   d) Jharkhand

6. Which of these is the most densely populated hot desert in the world?
   a) Sahara
   b) Namib
   c) Thar
   d) Gobi
7. Naga Kund, Roop Tirth and Kapil Vyapi Kund are the famous ghats of which lake?
   a) Pushkar
   b) Dal
   c) Hussain Sagar
   d) Chilika
8. Which Indian river was referred to as Shatadru in Sanskrit?
   a) Saraswati
   b) Beas
   c) Chenab
   d) Sutlej
9. According to the Guinness Book of World Records, which is the world's lowest lying country?
   a) Germany
   b) Sri Lanka
   c) The Netherlands
   d) Nepal
10. Which is the first Indian state to see the sun rise?
    a) Mizoram
    b) Arunachal Pradesh
    c) West Bengal
    d) Maharashtra
11. Which city do the Kumbh Mela and Anand Bhavan, the home of the Nehrus, have in common?

a) Nashik
   b) Allahabad
   c) Ujjain
   d) Mumbai
12. Harmattan, Sirocco and Mistral are different types of which of these?
    a) Cyclones
    b) Tsunamis
    c) Winds
    d) Rivers
13. Which mountain range runs through seven South American countries?
    a) Atlas
    b) Andes
    c) Ural
    d) Alps
14. Which Indian state is bordered by Bhutan, China and Myanmar?
    a) Arunachal Pradesh
    b) Tripura
    c) West Bengal
    d) Andhra Pradesh
15. Which country's administrative centre is Putrajaya?
    a) Cambodia
    b) Malaysia
    c) Australia
    d) Sri Lanka
16. Which of these is a landlocked country?
    a) Sri Lanka
    b) Pakistan
    c) Nepal

d) Bangladesh
17. Khardung La, Zoji La and Jelep La are names of different...
    a) Lakes in Goa
    b) Mountain passes
    c) Deserts in India
    d) Districts of Kerala
18. Which port city is also home to the Eastern Naval Command of the Indian Navy?
    a) Visakhapatnam
    b) Kandla
    c) Kolkata
    d) Mumbai
19. Which of these rivers originates in India?
    a) Tigris
    b) Brahmaputra
    c) Hwang Ho
    d) Mahanadi
20. In which country would you get to see the 'Long Wall of Ten Thousand Li'?
    a) China
    b) Afghanistan
    c) Japan
    d) Thailand
21. Which of these states shares its border with Bangladesh?
    a) Andhra Pradesh
    b) Tripura
    c) Madhya Pradesh
    d) Maharashtra
22. What does the word 'Sahara' mean in Arabic?

a) Desert
b) River
c) Hill
d) Mirage

23. Dudhsagar, Hundru and Chitrakoot are names of...
    a) Deserts
    b) Mountains
    c) Waterfalls
    d) Glaciers

24. Which part of the human body does the hill station Nainital get its name from?
    a) Ears
    b) Eyes
    c) Lips
    d) Feet

25. Which river's tributaries are Jhelum, Chenab and Ravi?
    a) Indus
    b) Ganga
    c) Brahmaputra
    d) Krishna

MATHS-II

Please go sequentially from left to right (not following BODMAS)

You can use addition, subtraction, multiplication or division to figure out the correct answer:

1.	6		9		32		28	= 50
2.	34		2		28		8	= 12
3.	39		13		43		38	= 8
4.	40		20		5		1	= 11
5.	15		2		50		20	= 4
6.	3		97		55		3	= 15
7.	64		13		48		2	= 58
8.	85		5		20		13	= 24

HISTORY-I

1. Which historical place is a small village in the Navsari district of Gujarat?
   a) Chauri Chaura
   b) Malgudi
   c) Dandi
   d) Noakhali
2. In 1987, the Italian government approved a $25 million project to reduce the tilt of which monument?
   a) Leaning Tower of Pisa
   b) The Statue of Liberty
   c) Eiffel Tower
   d) Sydney Opera House
3. Mahatma Gandhi tried for many years, but what was finally found by Gangabehn Majmundar?
   a) The word 'Harijan'
   b) Wooden sandals
   c) Charkha
   d) Rimmed spectacles
4. What did the Raja of Sikkim gift the British on 1 February 1835?
   a) Mount Everest
   b) Kaziranga National Park
   c) Darjeeling
   d) Taj Mahal
5. Which of these Mughal emperors discouraged music and placed a ban upon it?
   a) Babur

b) Shah Jahan
   c) Aurangzeb
   d) Genghis Khan
6. What animal adorned most of Tipu Sultan's possessions?
   a) King cobra
   b) Butterfly
   c) Tiger
   d) Camel
7. Which monument is painted every seven years with approximately 60 tonnes of paint?
   a) Qutb Minar
   b) Taj Mahal
   c) Eiffel Tower
   d) Great Wall of China
8. Which famous Kathiawad-born person gave up wearing a shirt and cap from September 1921?
   a) Mowgli
   b) Tarzan
   c) Mahatma Gandhi
   d) King George VI
9. In which state is Chetak Samadhi, a memorial to Maharana Pratap's horse?
   a) Gujarat
   b) Rajasthan
   c) Maharashtra
   d) Madhya Pradesh
10. Which dynasty did Qutbuddin Aibak belong to?
    a) Slave
    b) Lodi
    c) Khilji

d) Maurya
11. In 1933, which of the following was first used in a pamphlet titled 'Now or Never'?
   a) Pakistan
   b) Bharat
   c) Inquilab
   d) Swaraj
12. Which Mughal emperor was the son of Princess Manmati?
   a) Babur
   b) Humayun
   c) Shah Jahan
   d) Ashoka
13. Who among these made broadcasts from the German-sponsored Azad Hind Radio from January 1942?
   a) Jawaharlal Nehru
   b) Subhas Chandra Bose
   c) Mahatma Gandhi
   d) Rabindranath Tagore
14. Who went to Natal in 1893 to serve a merchant named Dada Abdulla?
   a) Jawaharlal Nehru
   b) Mahatma Gandhi
   c) Vallabhbhai Patel
   d) Dhirubhai Ambani
15. Which king sent officers known as Dhamma Mahamattas to promote dharma throughout his empire?
   a) Ashoka
   b) Samudragupta
   c) Prithviraj Chauhan

d) Raja Raja Chola
16. In the mid-eighteenth century, French Commander Bussy made which landmark in Hyderabad his headquarters?
    a) Salar Jung Museum
    b) Golconda Fort
    c) Gol Gumbaz
    d) Charminar
17. Sheikh Mujibur Rahman was the first prime minister of which country?
    a) Afghanistan
    b) Bangladesh
    c) Sri Lanka
    d) Pakistan
18. Whose voyages of discovery have been immortalized in Portugal's patriotic poem, *The Lusiads*?
    a) Ibn Battuta
    b) Ferdinand Magellan
    c) Vasco da Gama
    d) Marco Polo
19. During which war did Joan of Arc lead the French army?
    a) Hundred Years' War
    b) French Revolution
    c) Kalinga War
    d) Crimean War
20. Who was the monarch of Great Britain when India became independent?
    a) Queen Anne
    b) Queen Victoria
    c) George VI

d) Elizabeth II
21. Who was the last Tirthankara of Jainism?
    a) Sathya Sai Baba
    b) Buddha
    c) Guru Nanak
    d) Mahavira
22. Which ancient north Indian city was called Mahodya?
    a) Kanyakumari
    b) Kannauj
    c) Kanpur
    d) Kolkata
23. In June 1885, what was brought to New York harbour in a French ship called Isere?
    a) Statue of Liberty
    b) Leaning Tower of Pisa
    c) Lincoln Memorial
    d) White House
24. Which monument has a diameter of 14.32 metres at the base and about 2.75 metres at the top?
    a) Lotus Temple
    b) Sanchi Stupa
    c) Qutb Minar
    d) Gol Gumbaz
25. After which of these wars was the League of Nations formed?
    a) World War I
    b) World War II
    c) Gulf War
    d) Vietnam War

FUN FACTS-3

1. The most valued topaz colours are orange-red to red. Blue gems are widely available.
2. Wimbledon has its own resident hawk named Rufus. His work is to deter local pigeons from the All England Club.
3. In India, Sushruta is regarded as the 'father of surgery'. He is said to have conducted complicated surgeries in different parts of the human body in ancient India.
4. In the *Hunger Games*, Katniss Everdeen used a three-fingered salute as a signal of rebellion against the Capitol. This salute is now being used by pro-democracy protesters in Thailand and Hong Kong.
5. One of the tallest known dinosaurs, *Sauroposeidon*, was taller than a five-storey building.
6. The Pacific Ocean gets its name from the Latin Mare Pacificum, meaning 'Peaceful Sea'.
7. Triskaidekaphobia is the fear of the number thirteen.
8. Before he became an actor, Arjun Kapoor was assistant director for several films such as *Shakti: The Power*, *Kal Ho Naa Ho* and *Salaam-e-Ishq*.
9. Helen Keller became blind and deaf before she was two years old. She still went on to learn how to speak, read and write, and graduated from college with honours.
10. The Greater Chennai Corporation is said to be the oldest municipal institution in India. It was established

on 29 September 1688.
11. In Assam, the first day of Rongali Bihu is dedicated to cattle and is celebrated as 'Goru Bihu'.
12. The human brain weighs about 1.4 kilograms.
13. The word pixel is an abbreviation of picture element.
14. The currency of Peru is called nuevo sol, Spanish for 'new sun'.
15. Sea stars, commonly called starfish, do not have a heartbeat because they do not have a heart.

HISTORY-II

1. The Humayun Gate and the Talaqi Gate are gateways of which monument?
   a) Purana Qila
   b) Jama Masjid
   c) Red Fort
   d) Taj Mahal
2. Whom did Daulat Khan, the governor of Lahore, invite to invade India?
   a) Genghis Khan
   b) Tamerlane
   c) Alexander
   d) Babur
3. According to legend, the great demand for whose ashes led to the creation of a water tank in Pawapuri?
   a) Mahavira
   b) Mahatma Gandhi
   c) Buddha
   d) Raj Kapoor
4. Which monument was built by Aurangzeb's son as a tribute to his mother Rabia Durani?
   a) Hawa Mahal
   b) Bibi Ka Maqbara
   c) Bara Imambara
   d) Gol Gumbaz
5. In which continent are the Pyramids of Giza located?
   a) Asia
   b) Europe

c) Africa
   d) Australia
6. Who is the famous son of Nosekeni Fanny from South Africa?
   a) Jacques Kallis
   b) Martin Luther King Jr.
   c) Ravi Shankar
   d) Nelson Mandela
7. Raja Raja I, the builder of the Brihadishvara Temple in Thanjavur, belonged to which dynasty?
   a) Chera
   b) Chola
   c) Pandya
   d) Maurya
8. What measures 1,500 km in length from Sonar Gaon in Bengal to the Sindhu River in the west?
   a) Ganges
   b) Deccan Plateau
   c) Grand Trunk Road
   d) Great Wall of China
9. Which of these was virtually forgotten until 1818, when General Taylor, a British officer, rediscovered it?
   a) Taj Mahal
   b) Sanchi
   c) Nalanda
   d) Uttar Pradesh
10. The Hawa Mahal is said to have been designed to resemble...
    a) Lord Krishna's crown
    b) The moon

c) Mount Everest
   d) A tabla
11. What was the title given to the chief minister in Shivaji's council of ministers?
   a) Peshwa
   b) Alamgir
   c) Chhatrapati
   d) Maharana
12. The Red Fort lies along which river?
   a) Yamuna
   b) Brahmaputra
   c) Narmada
   d) Godavari
13. It is believed that Ramchandra Pandurang came to be known by his popular name after Bajirao II gave him a...
   a) Cap
   b) Cannon
   c) Sword
   d) Horse
14. Which present-day city is the site of the historical cities of Tughlakabad and Shahjahanabad?
   a) Patna
   b) Kolkata
   c) Delhi
   d) Cuttack
15. Who did Mahatma Gandhi refer to as 'the one person in the world who can prevent a war'?
   a) Himself
   b) Napoleon
   c) The Pope

d) Adolf Hitler
16. Which religion did Ashoka convert to in the later part of his life?
    a) Buddhism
    b) Jainism
    c) Sikhism
    d) Bahaism
17. The Lion Capital of Sarnath is a specimen of the art of which dynasty?
    a) Gupta
    b) Maurya
    c) Maya
    d) Kushan
18. Which ruler of the Delhi Sultanate was a slave of Muhammad Ghori?
    a) Qutbuddin Aibak
    b) Muhammad bin Tughluq
    c) Balban
    d) Razia Sultan
19. Which monument are you most likely to see from the Sireh Deorhi Bazaar?
    a) Hawa Mahal
    b) Statue of Liberty
    c) Qutb Minar
    d) Leaning Tower of Pisa
20. Who hoisted the Indian flag at the Red Fort on 15 August 1947?
    a) Jawaharlal Nehru
    b) Indira Gandhi
    c) Vallabhbhai Patel
    d) Subhas Chandra Bose

21. Which Indian was the most famous son of Vishwanath Datta and Bhuvaneshwari Devi?
    a) Sri Chaitanya
    b) Sant Kabir
    c) Guru Ram Das
    d) Swami Vivekananda
22. Whose birth anniversary on 11 November is celebrated as National Education Day in India?
    a) Vallabhbhai Patel
    b) Maulana Abul Kalam Azad
    c) Bal Gangadhar Tilak
    d) Lala Lajpat Rai
23. How many storeys does the Hawa Mahal have?
    a) One
    b) Four
    c) Five
    d) Twenty
24. Who among these was the wife of a Mughal emperor?
    a) Rani Lakshmi Bai
    b) Razia Sultan
    c) Nur Jahan
    d) Joan of Arc
25. The Quwwat-ul-Islam Mosque is to the northeast of which monument?
    a) Victoria Memorial
    b) Taj Mahal
    c) Humayun's Tomb
    d) Qutb Minar

HUMAN BODY

1. Which organ in the human body generates the most heat?
   a) Eye
   b) Liver
   c) Kidney
   d) Heart
2. Which of these is the rarest blood group?
   a) AB negative
   b) O positive
   c) A positive
   d) B positive
3. The muscles of which organ are the busiest muscles in the human body?
   a) Eye
   b) Nose
   c) Ear
   d) Tongue
4. Which of these is caused by a sudden closure of the human glottis?
   a) Blink
   b) Yawn
   c) Sneeze
   d) Hiccup
5. Whose work on the smallpox vaccine was inspired by Blossom the cow?
   a) Alexander Fleming
   b) Louis Pasteur

c) Edward Jenner
   d) Alexander Graham Bell
6. According to the US National Library of Medicine, which is the second most common disorder?
   a) Tooth decay
   b) Cataract
   c) Pneumonia
   d) Headache
7. More than half of the bones in the human body are found in your...
   a) Hands and feet
   b) Ribs
   c) Face
   d) Ears
8. The jejunum and the ileum are parts of which of these in the human body?
   a) Stomach
   b) Liver
   c) Small intestine
   d) Large intestine
9. In which part of the body are the two sensory organs of balance located?
   a) Heart
   b) Ear
   c) Eye
   d) Nose
10. Among humans, which is the most common infection?
    a) Hepatitis B
    b) Eye infection
    c) Skin infection
    d) Common cold

11. Dermatology deals with the treatment of disorders of which of the following?
    a) Skin
    b) Heart
    c) Eyes
    d) Kidney
12. The colour of our eyes depends on the amount of melanin in the...
    a) Retina
    b) Iris
    c) Cornea
    d) Toenail
13. Where in the human body would you locate a hammer, anvil and stirrup?
    a) Eye
    b) Ear
    c) Nose
    d) Tongue
14. In the human body, the longest and strongest bones are found in the...
    a) Legs
    b) Heart
    c) Arms
    d) Head
15. How many ribs does a normal human being have?
    a) Twenty-four
    b) Thirty
    c) Forty-one
    d) Forty-five
16. In the Type 1 of which disease does the human body not make enough insulin?

a) Diabetes
   b) Jaundice
   c) Swine flu
   d) Malaria
17. The primary function of the hyoid bone in the human body is to support the...
    a) Appendix
    b) Thigh
    c) Big toe
    d) Tongue
18. Hepatitis is the inflammation of which organ of the human body?
    a) Eye
    b) Liver
    c) Brain
    d) Lungs
19. Which part of the human body has the thinnest skin?
    a) Lips
    b) Eyelids
    c) Palm
    d) Nose
20. Which of these measures about 20 feet in length in the human body?
    a) Large intestine
    b) Stomach
    c) Small intestine
    d) Liver
21. Renal diseases are also called...
    a) Kidney diseases
    b) Heart diseases
    c) Liver diseases

d) Lung diseases
22. In the human body, the primary function of which organ is to remove waste and excess water?
    a) Heart
    b) Liver
    c) Large intestine
    d) Kidney
23. The shape of the stomach in the human body resembles which letter?
    a) C
    b) J
    c) S
    d) T
24. Who would you consult if you were affected by 'caries'?
    a) Dermatologist
    b) Pulmonologist
    c) Dentist
    d) Hepatologist
25. Which is the most commonly tested part of the body?
    a) Heart
    b) Blood
    c) Liver
    d) Eyes

MATHS-III

Please go sequentially from left to right (not following BODMAS)

You can use addition, subtraction, multiplication or division to figure out the correct answer:

1.	72		46		4		8	=	13
2.	8		12		26		14	=	5
3.	21		3		24		12	=	19
4.	23		8		74		11	=	10
5.	46		24		3		5	=	71
6.	84		47		7		22	=	2
7.	43		10		19		2	=	17
8.	25		3		14		54	=	35

NATURE AND WILDLIFE

1. According to legend, the absence of which insect gave the Silent Valley National Park in Kerala its name?
   a) Mosquito
   b) Firefly
   c) Cicada
   d) Honeybee
2. A species of which bird is the fastest underwater swimming bird?
   a) Penguin
   b) Pelican
   c) Kingfisher
   d) Hummingbird
3. What makes the African pygmy squirrel special?
   a) It is the smallest squirrel
   b) It is the heaviest squirrel
   c) It is the largest squirrel
   d) It is the largest mammal
4. Which of these animals does not have spots on its body?
   a) Giraffe
   b) Chital
   c) Sangai
   d) Dalmatian
5. Of these four breeds of dogs, which is the tallest?
   a) Pug
   b) Great Dane
   c) Labrador

d) Irish Wolfhound
6. In 1830, the northern boundary of which forest in Asia came to be known as the Dampier-Hodge's Line?
   a) Sunderbans
   b) Kaziranga
   c) Nottingham
   d) Gir
7. In which state is the Khangchendzonga National Park located?
   a) Sikkim
   b) Goa
   c) Tamil Nadu
   d) Uttar Pradesh
8. Tipu Sultan developed a special breed of what, called Hallikar, to transport heavy weapons?
   a) Cattle
   b) Elephant
   c) Cat
   d) Giraffe
9. In India, what do the two breeds of goat, Changra and Chegu, produce?
   a) Pashmina
   b) Merino wool
   c) Silk
   d) Velvet
10. Which is the heaviest living bird in the world?
    a) Hummingbird
    b) Ostrich
    c) Crane
    d) Albatross
11. Its natural habitat is in a small part of China, but the

Chinese name for this animal translates to 'large bear-cat'. Which one of the following is it?
a) Porcupine
b) Raccoon
c) Giant panda
d) Koala

12. Cuttlefish have...
a) W-shaped pupils
b) Twelve stomachs
c) Fourteen hearts
d) No bones

13. What is the name of Joy Adamson's first novel based on the life of a lion cub?
a) *Pippa's Challenge*
b) *Born Free*
c) *The Searching Spirit*
d) *Queen of Sheba*

14. Macropus gigantius, meaning 'big foot', is the scientific name of...
a) Kangaroo
b) Giraffe
c) Giant panda
d) Zebra

15. Which country is home to nine out of ten of the world's orangutans?
a) China
b) Indonesia
c) Kenya
d) South Africa

16. Barasingha is a type of...
a) Mouse

b) Elephant
   c) Deer
   d) Lion
17. The majority of police dogs in the world are...
   a) Dalmatians
   b) German Shepherds
   c) Chihuahuas
   d) Labradors
18. Sahiwal, Ongole, Red Sindhi and Jersey are different breeds of which animal?
   a) Goats
   b) Horses
   c) Blue whales
   d) Cows
19. What is the colour of the blood of an octopus?
   a) Blue
   b) Green
   c) Red
   d) Yellow
20. Which animal is called 'ora', or 'land crocodile' by the locals in Indonesia?
   a) Giant panda
   b) Komodo dragon
   c) King cobra
   d) Chimpanzee
21. Which is the oldest national park in India?
   a) Yellowstone National Park
   b) Gir National Park
   c) Kaziranga National Park
   d) Jim Corbett National Park
22. A shrimp's heart is located in its...

a) Head
b) Legs
c) Hands
d) Liver

23. Which of these creatures does not have a blood system?
    a) Hippopotamus
    b) Jellyfish
    c) Frog
    d) Shark

24. Black mambas get their name from the blue-black colour of their...
    a) Pupils
    b) Skin
    c) Inside of the mouth
    d) Fangs

25. Which country is the breeding ground of 60 per cent of the world's Atlantic puffins?
    a) Iceland
    b) Canada
    c) Nepal
    d) Brazil

POLITICS

1. Which country had the first woman prime minister in the world?
   a) India
   b) Sri Lanka
   c) United Kingdom
   d) Pakistan
2. In the 1990s, which former prime minister of India lost to Vijay Kumar Malhotra in a parliamentary election?
   a) Manmohan Singh
   b) Rajiv Gandhi
   c) Indira Gandhi
   d) Lal Bahadur Shastri
3. Who was the first chairman of the Rajya Sabha to serve for two terms?
   a) Dr S. Radhakrishnan
   b) Jawaharlal Nehru
   c) Vallabhbhai Patel
   d) Dr B.R. Ambedkar
4. Who among these members of the Nehru/Gandhi family lived the longest?
   a) Rajiv Gandhi
   b) Jawaharlal Nehru
   c) Indira Gandhi
   d) Sanjay Gandhi
5. What did A.B. Vajpayee add to Lal Bahadur Shastri's slogan 'Jai Jawan, Jai Kisan' ?

a) Jai Sultan
b) Jai Vigyan
c) Jai Hindustan
d) Jai Sangram

6. Who succeeded Rajiv Gandhi as the prime minister of India?
   a) Dr Manmohan Singh
   b) Lal Bahadur Shastri
   c) Jawaharlal Nehru
   d) V.P. Singh

7. Which Indian president's title was 'Giani'?
   a) S. Radhakrishnan
   b) Zail Singh
   c) Rajendra Prasad
   d) A.P.J. Abdul Kalam

8. Who is the longest-serving woman chief minister in India?
   a) Jayalalithaa
   b) Mamata Banerjee
   c) Sheila Dikshit
   d) Mayawati

9. How many people served as president of the USA in the eighteenth century?
   a) One
   b) Two
   c) Three
   d) Four

10. V.V. Giri, F.A. Ahmed and Neelam Sanjiva Reddy were all...
    a) Prime ministers of India
    b) Presidents of India

c) Chief Election Commissioners
   d) Governors of RBI
11. Who was the first serving president of India to cast a vote in a general election?
    a) N. Sanjiva Reddy
    b) K.R. Narayanan
    c) Zail Singh
    d) Zakir Hussain
12. The Rashtrapati Bhavan in Delhi was the erstwhile residence of the British...
    a) Governor-general
    b) Viceroy
    c) Prime minister
    d) Queen
13. Who wrote the book *Painting as a Pastime*?
    a) Adolf Hitler
    b) Albert Einstein
    c) Winston Churchill
    d) Mahatma Gandhi
14. Who was the first Indian president to visit the world's highest battlefield, the Siachen Glacier?
    a) Pratibha Patil
    b) A.P.J. Abdul Kalam
    c) Pranab Mukherjee
    d) No Indian president has visited it
15. Which Indian prime minister was born in Mughalsarai, Uttar Pradesh?
    a) Lal Bahadur Shastri
    b) Morarji Desai
    c) Indira Gandhi
    d) Rajiv Gandhi

16. Veer Bhoomi is the memorial to which Indian prime minister?
    a) Indira Gandhi
    b) Rajiv Gandhi
    c) Jawaharlal Nehru
    d) Lal Bahadur Shastri
17. In 1937, which Indian prime minister wrote an essay in *The Modern Review* of Calcutta under the pen-name Chanakya?
    a) Lal Bahadur Shastri
    b) Indira Gandhi
    c) Jawaharlal Nehru
    d) P.V. Narasimha Rao
18. Which American president gave the 'White House' its official name?
    a) Franklin Roosevelt
    b) Abraham Lincoln
    c) Gerald Ford
    d) Theodore Roosevelt
19. Who among the following prime ministers is not a recipient of the Bharat Ratna?
    a) Lal Bahadur Shastri
    b) Rajiv Gandhi
    c) Indira Gandhi
    d) V.P. Singh
20. In 2011, who became the chief minister of Tamil Nadu?
    a) Sushma Swaraj
    b) Sheila Dikshit
    c) Mayawati
    d) J. Jayalalithaa

21. Who was the US president when Neil Armstrong set foot on the moon?
    a) Richard Nixon
    b) J.F. Kennedy
    c) Abraham Lincoln
    d) George W. Bush
22. In 2008, who received the first copy of the e-passport in India?
    a) Priyanka Chopra
    b) Pratibha Patil
    c) Sonia Gandhi
    d) Sachin Tendulkar
23. What is the minimum age required to be a member of the Rajya Sabha?
    a) 20 years
    b) 30 years
    c) 40 years
    d) 50 years
24. In India, which of these posts has never been held by a woman?
    a) President
    b) Vice-president
    c) Prime minister
    d) Chief minister
25. Which leader's father was a senior economist for the government of Kenya?
    a) Angela Merkel
    b) Sheikh Hasina
    c) Barack Obama
    d) Aung San Suu Kyi

26. In the 2014 general elections, which Lok Sabha constituency had the least number of voters?
    a) Lakshadweep
    b) Daman and Diu
    c) Puducherry
    d) South Goa

FUN FACTS-4

1. Premchand, the author of the famous works *Rangmanch* and *Ghaban*, started his literary career as a freelancer in Urdu. He switched to Hindi in 1914–15.
2. The Dalai Lama is generally referred to as Yeshe Norbu or the 'Wish Fulfilling Gem' by the Tibetans.
3. The largest religious structure ever built is Angkor Wat in Cambodia. Dedicated to the Hindu god Vishnu, it is spread over an area of 401 acres.
4. In 2001, Dennis Tito, a 61-year-old former NASA engineer, became the first paying space tourist in the world.
5. Mamenchisaurus had the longest neck of any animal that ever lived. It was more than 9 metres in length.
6. Nearly eight out of ten people in the world speak only 1 per cent of the languages in the world.
7. The world's lowest and highest points are located in Asia. The lowest, the Dead Sea, is 422 m below sea level. The highest, Mt. Everest, is more than 8 km above sea level.
8. As a child, the famous runner Wilma Rudolph suffered from polio and could not walk without her orthopaedic shoe. At the 1960 Olympics, she became the first American woman ever to win three gold medals in one year.
9. After visiting the Kumbh Mela of 1895, Mark Twain wrote, 'It is wonderful, the power of a faith like that, that can make multitudes upon multitudes

of the old and weak and the young and frail enter without hesitation or complaint upon such incredible journeys...'
10. The first floor of the Charminar was used as a madarasa (college) during the Qutub Shahi period.
11. West Bengal is famous for its Baluchari sarees. Produced in the Murshidabad district of the state, these sarees mostly depict stories from the ancient texts and epics of India.
12. The margherita pizza is said to represent the colours in the Italian flag: red, tomatoes; green, basil; and white, cheese.
13. The Ojibwe, a group of indigenous people in North America, hang a dream catcher over a baby's cradle to filter out bad dreams.
14. Dilip Kumar won the Filmfare Award for Best Actor for three years in a row, for *Azaad*, *Devdas* and *Naya Daur*.
15. The young ones of porcupines are called porcupettes.

SCIENCE AND TECHNOLOGY

1. According to Albert Einstein, _____ is more important than knowledge.' Fill in the blank.
   a) Education
   b) Learning
   c) Imagination
   d) Intelligence
2. Which planet was known in ancient Greece by two different names—Phosphorus when it appeared as a morning star and Hesperus when it appeared as an evening star?
   a) Venus
   b) Mercury
   c) Jupiter
   d) Mars
3. The official name of Twitter's bird is...
   a) Sandy
   b) Larry
   c) Jordan
   d) Jack
4. What name did its inventor choose for it, preferring this name over Mesh and The Information Mine?
   a) Laptop
   b) Malware
   c) Mouse
   d) World Wide Web
5. Which of these can you type using the top set of letters on a standard keyboard?

a) EUROPE
b) ASIA
c) AFRICA
d) NORTH AMERICA

6. Apart from Uranus, which planet was discovered after the invention of the telescope?
   a) Neptune
   b) Venus
   c) Jupiter
   d) Earth

7. Which of these elements is named after a country?
   a) Curium
   b) Indium
   c) Francium
   d) Osmium

8. .af is the internet code of which country?
   a) Angola
   b) Australia
   c) Afghanistan
   d) Bhutan

9. Uranus gets its blue-green colour because of the presence of which gas?
   a) Methane
   b) Ammonia
   c) Chlorine
   d) Bromine

10. The steam engine, invented by James Watt, was initially used for...
    a) Ironing clothes
    b) Pumping water
    c) Mowing grass

d) Boiling potatoes
11. Which of the following would you find on the logo of the application Instagram?
    a) Hummingbird
    b) Lightning bolt
    c) Clock
    d) Camera
12. In 2003, METSAT or India's meteorological series of satellites was renamed after whom?
    a) Rakesh Sharma
    b) Kalpana Chawla
    c) Edmund Hillary
    d) Arundhati Roy
13. A Sukhoi-30 took off on 25 November 2009 from Pune. Which famous person was on board?
    a) M.S. Dhoni
    b) Pratibha Patil
    c) A.P.J. Abdul Kalam
    d) Aishwarya Rai
14. Which of these reflects the most sunlight?
    a) Green forests
    b) Sand desert
    c) Land covered with snow
    d) Oceans
15. Which key usually appears between the 'Alt' keys on a 'Qwerty' keyboard?
    a) Enter
    b) Space bar
    c) Tab
    d) Shift
16. Which is the farthest planet from Earth that can be

observed unaided by the human eye?
a) Jupiter
b) Saturn
c) Neptune
d) Mars

17. Which of these takes the most time to break down during waste disposal?
a) Paper napkin
b) Tin can
c) Glass bottle
d) Nylon fabric

18. Which of the following appear when a person has read a message sent on WhatsApp?
a) Blue ticks
b) Blue hearts
c) Blue circles
d) Blue lines

19. Which of these scientific units is not named after a person?
a) Hertz
b) Pascal
c) Candela
d) Watt

20. Which function key activates the 'Help' menu on a standard computer keyboard?
a) F4
b) F3
c) F2
d) F1

21. Which ancient branch of Indian medicine means 'Knowledge of Life' in Sanskrit?

a) Ayurveda
   b) Homeopathy
   c) Reiki
   d) Acupuncture
22. Which of these gases is commonly used to disinfect water and is part of the sanitation process for sewage and industrial waste?
   a) Ammonia
   b) Hydrogen
   c) Chlorine
   d) Helium
23. Which computer game features ghosts such as Blinky, Inky, Pinky and Clyde?
   a) Subway Surfers
   b) Temple Run
   c) Candy Crush
   d) Pac-Man
24. In Twitter, what do the letters 'RT' stand for?
   a) Real Tweet
   b) Run Time
   c) Retweet
   d) Repeat Tweet
25. In 1696, who became the warden of the Royal Mint of Great Britain?
   a) Archimedes
   b) Charles Darwin
   c) Isaac Newton
   d) Alfred Nobel

SPORTS-I

1. When a cricket umpire touches both shoulders with opposite hands in front of him, what is he signalling?
   a) Change of decision
   b) One run short
   c) Dead ball
   d) There is no such signal
2. In 1972, which colour was introduced for tennis balls, to make them more visible on TV?
   a) Green
   b) Yellow
   c) Black
   d) Orange
3. Which is the smallest country to have hosted the Summer Olympic Games?
   a) Greece
   b) Finland
   c) Sweden
   d) China
4. Till 2016, who has captained India for the most number of ODIs?
   a) Mohammad Azharuddin
   b) Sourav Ganguly
   c) M.S. Dhoni
   d) Sachin Tendulkar
5. Among Indians, who held the record of scoring the most number of runs in Twenty20 Internationals at the end of 2016?

a) Gautam Gambhir
   b) Virender Sehwag
   c) Virat Kohli
   d) Harbhajan Singh
6. In Test cricket, which of these Indians has scored the most hundreds against the same country?
   a) Sunil Gavaskar
   b) Sachin Tendulkar
   c) Bishen Singh Bedi
   d) Rahul Dravid
7. Which of these is true if a player is in his own half in an international football match?
   a) Can handle the ball
   b) Can stop a player with a hand
   c) Cannot be ruled offside
   d) Cannot be red-carded
8. Till 2016 who among these had played the most number of Test matches?
   a) Shane Warne
   b) M. Muralitharan
   c) Courtney Walsh
   d) Anil Kumble
9. Which is the only Grand Slam tennis tournament to have been played on three surfaces: grass, clay and hard court?
   a) Australian Open
   b) US Open
   c) Wimbledon
   d) French Open
10. What is the name of the Formula One Grand Prix track in India?

a) Lakshman International Circuit
b) Krishna International Circuit
c) Mahavir International Circuit
d) Buddh International Circuit

11. In ODIs, who was adjudged Man of the Match the maximum number of times till 2016?
    a) Sachin Tendulkar
    b) Ricky Ponting
    c) Sanath Jayasuriya
    d) Jacques Kallis

12. Among Indians, who has scored the most runs from fours and sixes in a single Test innings till 2016?
    a) M.S. Dhoni
    b) Virender Sehwag
    c) Sachin Tendulkar
    d) Sourav Ganguly

13. Against which team does Australia play the Ashes?
    a) England
    b) India
    c) Bangladesh
    d) Bhutan

14. Which wicketkeeper holds the Indian record for the most dismissals in ODls?
    a) Rahul Dravid
    b) Ranveer Singh
    c) Syed Kirmani
    d) M.S. Dhoni

15. In Davis Cup doubles, who has won the most consecutive matches without losing?
    a) Mahesh Bhupathi & Leander Paes
    b) Somdev Devvarman & Yuki Bhambri

c) Rohan Bopanna & Aisam-ul-Haq Qureshi
   d) Zeeshan Ali & Anand Amritraj
16. Who scored the first ODI century for India?
    a) Sunil Gavaskar
    b) Yuvraj Singh
    c) Kapil Dev
    d) Virender Sehwag
17. In Test cricket, which is the only team to have lost five wickets for no runs thrice in a Test innings?
    a) India
    b) Bangladesh
    c) New Zealand
    d) Pakistan
18. In 2005, who became India's first Formula One racing driver?
    a) Vijender Singh
    b) Vijay Mallya
    c) Narain Karthikeyan
    d) Karun Chandhok
19. Which Olympic sport takes place on a mat called 'tatami', with the contest lasting five minutes?
    a) Karate
    b) Judo
    c) Boxing
    d) Wrestling
20. In cricket, what is a 'golden duck'?
    a) When a batsman is out on a duck in the second innings of a Test
    b) When a batsman is out on the first ball he faces
    c) When a batsman scores 0 in both innings of a Test
    d) When a batsman remains unbeaten on 0

21. The national stadium located in which of these cities is nicknamed the 'Bird's Nest'?
    a) Beijing
    b) Paris
    c) New Delhi
    d) London
22. Till 2016, who held the Indian record of hitting the maximum number of sixes in a T20 International career?
    a) Harbhajan Singh
    b) Kapil Dev
    c) Yusuf Pathan
    d) Yuvraj Singh
23. Who is the first Indian to have scored a century during his World Cup debut?
    a) Anil Kumble
    b) C.K. Nayudu
    c) Virat Kohli
    d) Suresh Raina
24. Which state is known for the martial art form Kalaripayattu?
    a) Tamil Nadu
    b) Kerala
    c) Karnataka
    d) Maharashtra
25. In cricket, who is the only Indian to have scored five hundreds in five consecutive Test matches?
    a) Virender Sehwag
    b) Gautam Gambhir
    c) Sachin Tendulkar
    d) Harbhajan Singh

MATHS-IV

Please go sequentially from left to right (not following BODMAS)

You can use addition, subtraction, multiplication or division to figure out the correct answer:

1.	19		5		14		9	=	9
2.	18		9		26		25	=	27
3.	13		5		41		3	=	8
4.	38		12		34		4	=	15
5.	9		7		5		12	=	70
6.	42		7		7		14	=	98
7.	26		18		3		35	=	59
8.	56		14		25		9	=	5

SPORTS-II

1. Which sport is the term 'silly point' associated with?
   a) Kho Kho
   b) Cricket
   c) Kabaddi
   d) Football
2. In the history of the FIFA World Cup, Lucien Laurent of France was the first player to...
   a) Be red-carded
   b) Be substituted
   c) Score a goal
   d) Referee a match
3. Who is the first player to score a century on his debut in the Ranji Trophy, Duleep Trophy and Irani Trophy?
   a) Sunil Gavaskar
   b) Sachin Tendulkar
   c) Irfan Pathan
   d) Virender Sehwag
4. Excluding friendlies, who has scored the maximum number of goals for FC Barcelona in all competitions?
   a) Ronaldinho
   b) Lionel Messi
   c) Neymar
   d) Cesc Fabregas
5. Among left-handed batsmen, who has scored the most Test runs for India?
   a) Ajit Wadekar

b) Yuvraj Singh
   c) Ravi Shastri
   d) Sourav Ganguly
6. What kind of a creature was Fuleco, the mascot for the 2014 World Cup?
   a) Three-banded armadillo
   b) Olive Ridley turtle
   c) Green anaconda
   d) Giant panda
7. Who received the Rajiv Gandhi Khel Ratna Award in 2011?
   a) Akshay Kumar
   b) Sushil Kumar
   c) Gagan Narang
   d) M.S. Dhoni
8. Which team won the English Premier League in its inaugural year (1992–93)?
   a) Manchester United
   b) Newcastle United
   c) Arsenal
   d) Blackburn Rovers
9. Which of these sportspersons has not had a biopic based on him/her?
   a) M.C. Mary Kom
   b) Milkha Singh
   c) Sania Mirza
   d) Paan Singh Tomar
10. After Sachin Tendulkar, who has scored the most runs in Test cricket?
    a) S. Chanderpaul
    b) Virender Sehwag

c) Ricky Ponting
   d) K. Sangakkara
11. How many times has India won the ICC Cricket World Cup?
    a) Once
    b) Twice
    c) Thrice
    d) Six times
12. Which team has played the maximum number of ODIs till 2016?
    a) India
    b) New Zealand
    c) Pakistan
    d) England
13. The Olympic Charter limits the duration of the Olympic Games to how many days?
    a) 16
    b) 18
    c) 20
    d) 21
14. Which of these sports is played in three variations—horse, cycle and elephant?
    a) Boxing
    b) Polo
    c) Weightlifting
    d) Snooker
15. What is the traditional colour of the jersey of the Indian national football team?
    a) Sky blue
    b) Green
    c) White

d) Red
16. Ken Aston, a football referee, was inspired by traffic lights to start which of the following?
    a) Yellow and red cards
    b) Different coloured jerseys
    c) Red and green footballs
    d) Coloured flags
17. Hook, jab and uppercut are punches used in which sport?
    a) Boxing
    b) Shooting
    c) Karate
    d) Judo
18. In 1920, a two-member squad consisting of P.C. Banerjee and P.F. Chaugle represented India at the Olympic Games. Which discipline did they perform in?
    a) Athletics
    b) Swimming
    c) Gymnastics
    d) Wrestling
19. Who is the first Asian player to win a Grand Slam singles title?
    a) Sania Mirza
    b) Peng Shuai
    c) Li Na
    d) Ayumi Morita
20. In which sport at the 2012 London Olympics did India win a medal for the first time ever?
    a) Wrestling
    b) Hockey

c) Shooting
   d) Badminton
21. Which city's IPL team bears the name 'Sunrisers'?
   a) Bengaluru
   b) Hyderabad
   c) Chennai
   d) Kolkata
22. Deepika Kumari, Bombayla Devi Laishram and Laxmirani Majhi play which sport?
   a) Archery
   b) Badminton
   c) Volleyball
   d) Swimming
23. Which country won the most number of gold medals at the 2016 Summer Olympic Games?
   a) USA
   b) China
   c) Great Britain
   d) Russia
24. Till 2016, which cricketer had bowled the maximum number of balls for India in T20 Internationals?
   a) Harbhajan Singh
   b) Ravindra Jadeja
   c) Ravichandran Ashwin
   d) Umesh Yadav
25. Till 2016, which Indian had scored the most Test hundreds in a calendar year?
   a) Sachin Tendulkar
   b) M.S. Dhoni
   c) V.V.S. Lakshman
   d) Virat Kohli

TRAVEL

1. In 2006, the governor of Karnataka was requested to rename the Chennai-Mysore train service as...
   a) Maratha Express
   b) Malgudi Express
   c) Coffee Express
   d) Vidhana Soudha Express
2. Travelling from north to south, which of the following places will you reach last?
   a) Patna
   b) Darjeeling
   c) Panaji
   d) Nagpur
3. In which Indian state is Biju Patnaik Airport located?
   a) West Bengal
   b) Odisha
   c) Madhya Pradesh
   d) Punjab
4. Which of these is a UNESCO World Heritage Site?
   a) Hawa Mahal
   b) Charminar
   c) Fatehpur Sikri
   d) Gateway of India
5. In which state is the Nagaur Fair held?
   a) Rajasthan
   b) Gujarat
   c) Punjab
   d) Haryana

6. Which famous person has the SSPN railway station at Puttaparthi been named after?
   a) Sri Aurobindo
   b) Indira Gandhi
   c) M.S. Dhoni
   d) Sathya Sai Baba
7. The train 'Chetak Express' starts from Delhi. What is its last stop?
   a) Meerut
   b) Udaipur
   c) Jhansi
   d) Jaipur
8. The Pashupatinath Temple is located in which neighbouring country of India?
   a) Bangladesh
   b) Nepal
   c) Afghanistan
   d) China
9. Which one of these monuments is located in a state capital?
   a) Gol Gumbaz
   b) Charminar
   c) Meenakshi Temple
   d) Golden Temple
10. The train Vivek Express starts from Dibrugarh in Assam. What is its last stop?
    a) Madurai
    b) Mumbai
    c) Udhampur
    d) Kanyakumari
11. If you landed at Sardar Vallabhbhai Patel Airport,

which city would you have landed in?
a) New Delhi
b) Mumbai
c) Chennai
d) Ahmedabad

12. Which one of these states does not have a single UNESCO World Heritage Site?
a) Maharashtra
b) Uttar Pradesh
c) Bihar
d) Nagaland

13. The international airport in Nagpur is named after which former law minister of India?
a) B.R. Ambedkar
b) Maulana Azad
c) Mahatma Gandhi
d) Dr Rajendra Prasad

14. Which was the first mode of transport to appear on a stamp of independent India?
a) Aeroplane
b) Submarine
c) Car
d) Rickshaw

15. The luxury train Deccan Odyssey is a joint venture between Indian Railways and the government of...
a) Tamil Nadu
b) Odisha
c) Maharashtra
d) Uttar Pradesh

16. If you are travelling on Indian Railways with the ticket code 'CC', then you are travelling in…

a) AC 2 Tier
b) AC Chair Car
c) First Class
d) Sleeper Class

17. Which state would you be travelling to if you went through the tourist routes called Beas circuit, Dhauladhar circuit, Sutlej circuit and Tribal circuit?
    a) West Bengal
    b) Himachal Pradesh
    c) Odisha
    d) Rajasthan

18. The name of which train means 'non-stop' or 'fast' in Bengali?
    a) Rajdhani
    b) Shatabdi
    c) Duronto
    d) Garib Rath

19. In Indian Railways, what does the class code 'SL' stand for?
    a) Special
    b) Sleeper
    c) Slow
    d) Single

20. What is the source station of the Akal Takht Express?
    a) Amritsar
    b) Dwarka
    c) Patna
    d) Puri

21. In which state is the Nashik Kumbh Mela held?
    a) Kerala
    b) Maharashtra

c) Odisha
  d) Tamil Nadu
22. Which city is served by Chaudhary Charan Singh International Airport?
  a) Patna
  b) Dehradun
  c) Lucknow
  d) Raipur
23. What is the minimum age for an Indian passport?
  a) 15 years
  b) 18 years
  c) 21 years
  d) There is no minimum age
24. Most trains are named after which feature of the Indian landscape?
  a) Rivers
  b) Mountains
  c) Valleys
  d) Waterfalls
25. In 2001, Tirana airport in Albania was renamed after which Nobel laureate?
  a) Mahatma Gandhi
  b) Marie Curie
  c) Florence Nightingale
  d) Mother Teresa

BUZZER ROUND

SET-1

1. Which is heavier: 1,050 gm of cotton or 1 kg of iron?
2. Who served as the president of India from 1950 to 1962?
3. Which volcano in Japan last erupted in 1707?
4. Fill in the blank to complete the idiom: A _____ can't change its spots.
5. The first woman cosmonaut to receive the title of 'Hero of the Soviet Union' was...
6. The cerebrum is the largest part of which organ of the human body?
7. Param Vir Chakra may be given posthumously: serious or joking?
8. Which phrase, also the name of a film, means 'I have cut the kite', in Gujarati?
9. In which state is the Mamallapuram Dance Festival held?
10. Which word comes before 'Indians' in the name of an IPL team?

SET-2

1. In India, if a child had 'Do Boond Zindagi Ke', he or she would have been vaccinated for...
2. Which country is home to eight of the world's ten highest peaks?
3. The first name of which US president means 'the

blessed one' in Swahili?
4. Norah Jones is the daughter of which musician?
5. Orangutans spend most of their time on trees: serious or joking?
6. '.hk' is the internet country code for Hungary or Hong Kong?
7. Which one of these is a type of embroidery: kasuti or bidri?
8. Who said about whom: 'I only hope that we never lose sight of one thing—that it was all started by a mouse'?
9. The word yolk comes from the Old English word for which colour?
10. Which road in India was called the 'Long Walk' by European travellers?

SET-3

1. 'The Investigation of the State of Aether in Magnetic Fields' was the first 'scientific paper' of which physicist?
2. Who is the only British prime minister to receive a Nobel Prize for Literature?
3. The Padma Awards are given in three categories: Padma Vibhushan, Padma Bhushan and Padma...
4. Which is the first month of the Gregorian calendar to have thirty-one days?
5. In which language was the Rig Veda composed?
6. The taxonomic name of which animal means 'sea bear'?
7. In which state did Tanjore paintings originate?
8. Which Hindi film actor is popularly called Dabangg Khan?

9. Which landmark is located in Mumbai: Gateway of India or India Gate?
10. Which Indian hockey player's autobiography is titled *Goal*?

SET-4

1. Babur's tomb is located in which modern-day country?
2. Which word is common to a part of the face, the muzzle of a gun and the place where a river enters the sea?
3. Which cricketer took oath as a Rajya Sabha member in 2012?
4. Starfish do not have a brain: serious or joking?
5. Which actress has the nickname Bebo?
6. In India, does Beating the Retreat mark the end of the Republic Day celebrations or the Independence Day celebrations?
7. How many lines does a sonnet consist of?
8. The Chhatrapati Shivaji Terminus was built in 1887 to commemorate the golden jubilee of...
9. Who immediately preceded the only woman president of India?
10. In computers, what does 'Ctrl' stand for?

SET-5

1. Which gemstone now weighs 108.93 carats, having lost 43 per cent of its original weight?
2. Ne is the symbol of which chemical element?
3. Kimigayo is the national anthem of Japan or Indonesia?
4. In the animated TV series, who has the Omnitrix, a

watch-shaped device?
5. In which Indian state are the majority of Asiatic lions found?
6. In the fairy tale *The Ugly Duckling*, which bird does the duckling transform into?
7. Vinayak Chaturthi is held in honour of which Hindu deity?
8. The name of which vehicle comes from the Japanese words for 'man-powered carriage'?
9. Who is older: Anoushka Shankar or Norah Jones?
10. How many colours does the Olympic Flag have?

SET-6

1. If Babur was the first emperor of this dynasty, who was the last?
2. Which of these words comes from the Greek word for 'holding first place': protein or carbohydrate?
3. Alphabetically, the name of which month would come just after July?
4. The two horns of the black rhinoceros are made entirely of hardened…: enamel or hair?
5. Which animated character's main rival is the ten-year-old Kalia?
6. What, of national importance, was designed by D. Udaya Kumar?
7. Whose work is the train Godan Express named after?
8. A seismograph is an instrument that measures and records details of…
9. Jeev Milkha Singh has represented India in athletics at the Olympic Games: serious or joking?
10. In music, the concept of gharana emerged when

whose descendants decided to call themselves Seniyas?

SET-7

1. The Battle of Waterloo ended whose brief second reign?
2. Which word is common to a person who supervises or observes a process, and the screen of a computer?
3. A greater percentage of the Sunderbans mangrove forest lies in India or Bangladesh?
4. What kind of creature is Master Shifu in the film Kung Fu Panda?
5. Which state celebrates its formation day as Utkal Divas on April 1?
6. In Hamlet, who was Ophelia's father?
7. Vinson Massif is the highest point of which continent?
8. In cricket, what is 71.1 cm in height and 22.86 cm in width?
9. The word 'lunatic' comes from the Latin word for which heavenly body?
10. What does the 'S' in SIM card stand for?

SET-8

1. Rearrange the letters of the word 'trance' to get a word denoting a secretion from flowers.
2. If you were visiting the Sun Temple at Konark, which state would you be in?
3. Which metal was called platina del Pinto by the Spaniards for its resemblance to silver?
4. The name of which insect comes from the old French word for 'to crackle'?

5. What is the name of Chhota Bheem's pet monkey?
6. Which colour band of the National Flag of India does the chakra appear on?
7. 'A Mad Tea-Party' and 'The Lobster Quadrill' are chapters in which book?
8. The name of which mountain range of the Deccan Plateau means 'seven folds' in Hindi?
9. In 2010, who became the first fielder to take two hundred catches in Test matches?
10. In MS Word, if Ctrl+U is used to underline, then what is Ctrl+B used for?

SET-9

1. Aurangzeb and Humayun were emperors of which dynasty?
2. In AD 105, what was produced by Lun Tsai in China by mixing mulberry bark, hemp and rags with water?
3. Ozone is formed from which gas?
4. Which animal, apart from the emu, holds the shield on the Australian coat of arms?
5. Which word is common to Chacha Chaudhary's dog and a projectile?
6. In Indian Railways, what does the 'C' in 'RAC' stand for?
7. *The Pickwick Papers* was the first novel of which author?
8. Which is the last river to be mentioned in our national anthem?
9. Which badminton player received the Rajiv Gandhi Khel Ratna Award for the year 2010?

10. Which colour of the rainbow starts with the vowel between g and k?

SET-10

1. Whose house in Gwalior has become a museum called Sarod Ghar: Amjad Ali Khan or Zakir Hussain?
2. The Nobel Prize in Literature has never been shared by two people: serious or joking?
3. Which state was formerly called Rajputana?
4. The name of which element comes from a Greek word meaning 'something new'?
5. Which is the world's largest land carnivore: hippopotamus or polar bear?
6. Which colour on the national flag of India stands for light, the path of truth to guide our conduct?
7. Mannat is the name of which Hindi film actor's residence?
8. In literature, who went to Brobdingnag and Laputa?
9. Which numeric term is common to normal vision and a form of cricket?
10. The name of which South American country literally means 'little Venice'?

SET-11

1. Which musician was born as Robindro Shaunkor Chowdhury in Varanasi on 7 April 1920?
2. In 1840, what did Rowland Hill describe as 'a bit of paper...back with a glutinous wash'?
3. Which was the first planned city of the Mughals?
4. Rearrange the letters of the words 'art' and 'sun' to get the name of a planet.

5. Which American inventor founded a school in Boston in 1872, to train teachers of the deaf?
6. Which Indian award was given to Khan Abdul Ghaffar Khan in 1987 and to Nelson Mandela in 1990?
7. Giraffes have thirty-two teeth, just like you and me: serious or joking?
8. Which superhero's real name is Steve Rogers?
9. In which language did Premchand originally write *Godan*?
10. Which former athlete is sometimes referred to as Payyoli Express?

SET-12
1. Which Indian city is named after Jambu Lochan?
2. Which colour occupies the maximum area on the flag of China?
3. Which word was originally used as the telegraphic address of the International Criminal Police Commission?
4. The Mahesa-murti cave is the most important cave of which landmark?
5. Which mode of transport was once referred to as the 'iron horse': train or submarine?
6. Name the eldest son of former Uttar Pradesh chief minister Mulayam Singh Yadav.
7. The name of which species of deer sounds like a dish from southern India?
8. The financial year of India starts in June: serious or joking?
9. Who is also known as the Bard of Avon?
10. In the Olympic Games, which bird's feathers make

up the sixteen feathers in a shuttlecock used to play badminton?

SET-13

1. Which word is common to a substance used for sticking objects together and a part of the mouth?
2. What is the tomb of Arjumand Bano Begum better known as?
3. Who was the first of twelve men to walk on the surface of the moon?
4. Complete the name of this film: '_____ _____ and the Curse of Damyaan'.
5. Which animal appears on the seal of the Reserve Bank of India?
6. Yama, Niyam, Dhyan and Samadhi are four of the eightfold paths of what?
7. In a story by Premchand, which indoor game did Mirza Sajjad Ali and Mir Raushan Ali play?
8. Who was the first Indian sportsperson to have his statue in the famous Madame Tussauds museum?
9. Antarctica is the largest cold desert in the world: serious or joking?
10. Which word describes the centre of the target in archery and darts?

SET-14

1. Which award was created first: the Nobel Prize or the Ramon Magsaysay Award?
2. In which state are the Ajanta Caves located?
3. What did Joseph Priestley call it when he found that it rubbed out pencil marks?

4. In the Mahabharata, who was the youngest of the Pandavas?
5. According to the 2011 census, which state in India has the highest population?
6. Only male walruses have tusks: serious of joking?
7. In the fairy tale *Cinderella*, the fairy godmother turned which vegetable into a carriage?
8. A mushroom is a fungus: serious or joking?
9. Agatti, Amini, Andrott, Bitra, Chetlat are islands of which union territory?
10. Which colour is common to the flags of China, Nepal and Canada?

SET-15

1. Brihadratha, who was assassinated in 185 BCE, was which dynasty's last king?
2. Who played the male lead in *Rowdy Rathore*, *Thank You* and *Patiala House*?
3. Helium is named after the Greek word for hell: serious or joking?
4. Which festival is known as Fagu in Nepal?
5. Simba is the Swahili name of which animal?
6. In literature, who ended up in a London gang of thieves led by Fagin?
7. Which river is called Dihang in Arunachal Pradesh?
8. In which sport is the Golden Bails Award given?
9. The Ramon Magsaysay Award is named after the president of which country?
10. In Hindu mythology, who is called Muralidhar?

SET-16

1. What does the 'I' in 'FBI' stand for?
2. What in China begins at Shanhaiguan and ends at Jiayuguan?
3. Which of these awards honours Indian cinema: Jnanpith Award or Dadasaheb Phalke Award?
4. The planets Jupiter, Uranus, Neptune and Saturn all have rings: serious or joking?
5. The twenty-sixth state of India shares its name with which number?
6. Around 70 per cent of Brazil's total area comprises of the Amazon Rainforest: serious or joking?
7. In *The Jungle Book*, what kind of creature was Rikki Tikki Tavi?
8. If BCCI is associated with cricket in India, what is AIFF associated with?
9. Which type of silk accounts for about 90 per cent of the total production of silk in the world: mulberry or muga?
10. Whose portrait appeared on the Penny Black, the first stamp in the world?

SET-17

1. What was first rolled out in Kolkata on 24 February 1873?
2. Which city in Haryana was the site of three battles, fought in 1526, 1556, and 1761?
3. In *The Dark Knight Rises*, which superhero was played by Christian Bale?
4. Which woman received the Nobel Prize for Chemistry immediately before Victor Grignard and Paul Sabatier?

5. Butterflies are insects: serious or joking?
6. If Chaitra is the first month in the Saka calendar, which is the twelfth month?
7. Who is the narrator of Gulliver's Travels?
8. Which continent are Kenya, Uganda and Ghana located in?
9. Who is the first Indian bowler to take six hundred Test wickets?
10. Only oysters can produce pearls: serious or joking?

SET-18

1. What is produced by the insect Bombyx mori?
2. *Long Walk to* _____ is the title of Nelson Mandela's autobiography. Fill in the blank to complete its title.
3. Under whose directorship did the Physics department at IISc, Bangalore come into being in 1933?
4. How is Dharmendra related to actor Abhay Deol: father or uncle?
5. The first Indian Nobel Prize winner won the award in which category?
6. Which turtle found in Indian territory shares its name with an oil-bearing fruit?
7. Who came into the Seeonee Wolf Pack for a bull's price and on Baloo's good word?
8. Which is the only IPL team that has a number in its name?
9. Itanagar is named after Ita Fort meaning 'fort of bricks': serious or joking?
10. I am very heavy but backwards I'm not. Which word am I?

SET-19

1. Which is the only vowel that appears in the names of all the days of the week?
2. Which place, famous for its stupas, was known as Kakanaya in ancient times?
3. In the film *Stanley Ka Dabba*, what does 'dabba' specifically refer to?
4. In India, the birth anniversary of the eighth avatar of Lord Vishnu is celebrated as…
5. Only 50 per cent of an orangutan's genetic makeup is the same as a human's: serious or joking?
6. Which book written by Vishnu Sharma has five chapters?
7. A geographical feature rising more than 1,000 feet above its surrounding area is called a mountain or valley?
8. In cricket, the Border-Gavaskar Trophy is played between India and…?
9. A millennium refers to a period of how many years?
10. While writing in English, which planet has the letter 't' exactly in the middle of its name?

SET-20

1. How many months in the Gregorian calendar have thirty-one days?
2. Which Indian leader lends his name to a UNESCO World Heritage terminus in Mumbai?
3. Who is Aishwarya Rai's mother-in-law?
4. With which discovery would you associate Anna Bertha's hand, with its clearly visible bones?
5. Koalas are bears: serious or joking?

6. Which seven-letter word is common to the flower of Crocus sativus and the Indian flag?
7. Which Sanskrit poem's title translates as 'cloud–messenger'?
8. What is the winter capital of Jammu and Kashmir?
9. National Sports Day is celebrated in India on the birth anniversary of Milkha Singh or Dhyan Chand?
10. In a rainbow, if violet is at one extreme, which colour is at the other extreme?

SET-21

1. How many zeros have to be added to one million to make it ten lakh?
2. The life of which Indian ruler is known mainly through the works of Bana?
3. Which comic-strip character has a wife named Bini?
4. What is the national aquatic animal of India?
5. Which is the only astronomical body other than Earth ever visited by human beings?
6. Which play by William Shakespeare features the line, 'To be or not to be…'?
7. In which union territory of India would you find the naval base INS Dweeprakshak?
8. Who crossed Sourav Ganguly's record of twenty-one Test wins to become the most successful Test captain for India?
9. Which is the odd one out: heptagon, triangle, rectangle, cube, pentagon?
10. The king cobra can raise itself up to one-third of its body length: serious or joking?

SET-22

1. My mother's mother's only daughter is my...?
2. Which monument has more steps: Qutb Minar or Charminar?
3. In the film *My Name is Khan*, Christopher Duncan played the role of which president?
4. According to the Gregorian calendar, which national holiday in India is celebrated in the first month?
5. The guinea pig is a species of pig: serious or joking?
6. How many sides does a hexagon have?
7. What is the Scottish king Mac Bethad mac Findlaich better known as?
8. Which state is India's highest altitude zoological garden located in?
9. Which of these was not an event at the 2016 Olympic Games: judo or karate?
10. What used in everyday life gets wet when used for drying?

SET-23

1. In 2013, the lowest school dropout rate in India was in Kerala or Bihar?
2. Complete this quote by Gandhiji: 'Educate one man, you educate one person but educate a ____ and you educate a whole civilisation. '
3. A mirage can be seen only in a desert: serious or joking?
4. What is the scientific name of boa constrictor?
5. Which of these is a type of percussion instrument: xylophone or violin?
6. According to Hindu mythology, who is also known as Pawanputra?

7. In comics, which creature's bite granted Peter Parker incredible powers?
8. Which is the second largest state in India in terms of area?
9. How many bails are used in a cricket match?
10. The Bharat Ratna can only be awarded to Indians: serious or joking?

SET-24

1. In the acronym 'SAARC', what does 'R' stand for?
2. Who gave his first talk on a religious subject at a deer park in Sarnath?
3. What is the most abundant mineral in our body?
4. Despite its hump, a camel has a straight spine: serious or joking?
5. Which late singer was born as Jagmohan Singh in 1941?
6. In which state is the Nehru Trophy Boat Race held?
7. Which famous character, created by Charles Dickens, was married to Dora Spenlow?
8. The name of which continent means 'opposite to the Arctic'?
9. Which tennis championship is an annual event at Roland Garros?
10. 'March of the Volunteers' is the national anthem of which country?

SET-25

1. What replaced the king's portrait on the currency of Nepal in 2007?
2. Which Mughal emperor was the son of a Mughal

emperor but not the grandson of one?
3. In 1921, which Nobel Prize winner was given a gram of radium for her service to science?
4. Just like human beings, chimpanzees do not have hair on their palms and the soles of their feet: serious or joking?
5. In the 1975 film *Sholay*, which actor asked, 'Kitney aadmi thhey'?
6. In which state is the Surajkund Crafts Mela held?
7. If Hero is Phantom's horse, what kind of animal is Devil?
8. Which is the only state of India that starts with 'M' and ends with 'M'?
9. Bob, bun and crew are different styles of shoes or hairstyles?
10. At the Olympics, Dressage, Eventing and Jumping involve which animal?

ANSWERS

ART AND CULTURE

1. Santoor
2. Tamil Nadu
3. Amir Khusrau
4. Satyajit Ray
5. Zakir Hussain
6. Qatar
7. Krishna
8. Piano
9. Koodiyattam
10. Mridangam
11. Notes of Calssical music
12. Classical music
13. Amjad Ali Khan
14. Sa
15. Nawab Wajid Ali Shah
16. Green make-up
17. Horse
18. Mukhda
19. Mohiniattam
20. Amjad Ali Khan
21. A.R. Rahman
22. Ragas
23. Rangoli
24. Duffli
25. Gujarat

BOOKS and COMICS

1. Rabindranath Tagore
2. Garfield
3. Shylock
4. English
5. Perry Mason
6. Tenzing Norgay
7. Hobbes
8. Tarzan
9. Friday
10. *Treasure Island*
11. Robinson Crusoe Island
12. Hamlet
13. Jawaharlal Nehru
14. Ramayana
15. Batman
16. *Macbeth*
17. Portuguese
18. *Gulliver's Travels*
19. R.K. Laxman
20. Natkhat
21. Rig Veda
22. Sindbad
23. Woodcutter
24. Rani Lakshmi Bai
25. Vikramaditya

ENTERTAINMENT

1. Maine Pyar Kyun Kiya
2. Tiger
3. *Patiala House*

4. Amitabh Bachchan
5. Shahid Kapoor
6. *Parineeta*
7. *Singh is Kinng*
8. Aishwarya Rai
9. A.R. Rahman
10. Bhupen Hazarika
11. Shammi Kapoor
12. *My Name is Khan*
13. *Ek Tha Tiger*
14. Sonu Nigam
15. Hrithik Roshan
16. Akshay Kumar
17. Kamal Haasan
18. Salman Khan
19. Aishwarya Rai
20. Sridevi
21. Ashoka
22. Sonakshi Sinha
23. Amitabh Bachchan
24. Rajinikanth
25. Farhan Akhtar

FOOD-1

1. Pomegranate
2. Vada pav
3. Chilli
4. China
5. Popped popcorn
6. Brinjal
7. Potato

8. Sarson da saag
9. Tomato
10. Jalebi
11. Panipuri
12. Root
13. Jammu and Kashmir
14. Coffee
15. Orange
16. Pasta
17. Meat
18. Potato
19. Turmeric
20. Barfi
21. V. Kurien
22. Brazil
23. Coconut water
24. Jammu and Kashmir
25. Rasmalai

FOOD-II

1. Gulab jamun
2. Guava
3. Bhujia
4. Amla
5. Ginger
6. Chillies
7. Thukpa
8. Barfi
9. Okra
10. Kulfi
11. Poach

12. Sugar
13. Barfi
14. Saffron
15. Shawarma
16. Grapes
17. Paratha
18. Goa
19. Green
20. Alphonso
21. Boiling
22. Laddoo
23. Coriander
24. Bread crumbs
25. Chocolate; the Aztecs called chocolate 'xocoatl'.

GENERAL-I

1. Hair
2. Kiran Bedi
3. Santa Claus
4. Nelson Mandela
5. Indian sarees
6. Colon
7. Seven
8. Four. Woodrow Wilson, Theodore Roosevelt, Jimmy Carter, Barack Obama.
9. Gujarat. Hyderabad-9, Mumbai-6, Kavaratti-9, Gandhinagar-11 letters.
10. Head. This traditional headgear is made of strips of bamboo.
11. Hair colour
12. Literature

13. Passports
14. Paraguay
15. Goat
16. Nelson Mandela
17. Bhutan
18. India
19. Newspaper
20. White
21. Peace
22. USA. It has a population of 323,995,528.
23. Diamond
24. Coffee
25. Sherwani

MATHS-I

1.	30	Divide	6	Plus	4	Minus	8	=	1
2.	20	Plus	30	Multiply	4	Divide	25	=	8
3.	41	Plus	15	Minus	17	Divide	13	=	3
4.	60	Minus	24	Multiply	5	Divide	10	=	15
5.	45	Divide	3	Plus	10	Multiply	2	=	50
6.	55	Minus	34	Divide	7	Multiply	11	=	33
7.	25	Multiply	6	Minus	55	Divide	19	=	5
8.	67	Multiply	3	Minus	47	Divide	11	=	14

GENERAL-II

1. Pakistan
2. World Scout Committee
3. Nobel Prize
4. Knots per square inch
5. Ankle

6. Chinese
7. Three
8. Boat
9. Paper
10. Pleated salwars
11. Mother Teresa
12. Tea
13. India
14. Surma
15. Head
16. Six
17. 40
18. Clutch
19. Batik
20. Louis Braille
21. Tea bag
22. Four
23. Yemen
24. M.S. Subbulakshmi
25. Edmund Hillary

GENERAL-III
1. Embroidery
2. White
3. Slides down chimneys
4. Kerala
5. Nepal
6. Collars
7. Dragon
8. Ten thousand
9. Equals to

10. Chikankari
11. Green
12. Bandhni
13. Red
14. Achkan
15. Law
16. Mother Teresa
17. Cargos
18. United Nations
19. Myanmar
20. Hyderabad
21. Shoes
22. Wool; from the Persian word pašm.
23. Mauritius
24. China
25. Nylon

GEOGRAPHY

1. Kilimanjaro
2. Mumbai
3. Goa
4. Amazon Rainforest
5. Jharkhand
6. Thar
7. Pushkar
8. Sutlej
9. The Netherlands
10. Arunachal Pradesh
11. Allahabad
12. Winds
13. Andes. It is the longest continental mountain range in

the world.
14. Arunachal Pradesh
15. Malaysia
16. Nepal
17. Mountain passes
18. Visakhapatnam
19. Mahanadi
20. China
21. Tripura
22. Desert
23. Waterfalls
24. Eyes
25. Indus

MATHS-II

1.	6	Multiply	9	Minus	32	Plus	28	=	50
2.	34	Multiply	2	Plus	28	Divide	8	=	12
3.	39	Divide	13	Plus	43	Minus	38	=	8
4.	40	Plus	20	Divide	5	Minus	1	=	11
5.	15	Multiply	2	Plus	50	Divide	20	=	4
6.	3	Plus	97	Minus	55	Divide	3	=	15
7.	64	Plus	13	Minus	48	Multiply	2	=	58
8.	85	Divide	5	Plus	20	Minus	13	=	24

HISTORY-1

1. Dandi
2. Leaning Tower of Pisa
3. Charkha
4. Darjeeling
5. Aurangzeb
6. Tiger

7. Eiffel Tower
8. Mahatma Gandhi
9. Rajasthan
10. Slave
11. Pakistan
12. Shah Jahan
13. Subhas Chandra Bose
14. Mahatma Gandhi
15. Ashoka
16. Charminar
17. Bangladesh
18. Vasco da Gama
19. Hundred Years' War
20. George VI
21. Mahavira
22. Kannauj
23. Statue of Liberty
24. Qutb Minar. The construction was commenced by Qutbuddin Aibak and finished by Iltutmish.
25. World War I

HISTORY-II

1. Purana Qila. Bara Darwaza, Humayun Gate and Talaqi Gate are the three gateways.
2. Babur
3. Mahavira
4. Bibi Ka Maqbara
5. Africa
6. Nelson Mandela
7. Chola
8. Grand Trunk Road

9. Sanchi
10. Lord Krishna's crown
11. Peshwa
12. Yamuna
13. Cap. He was popularly known as Tantia Tope.
14. Delhi
15. Adolf Hitler
16. Buddhism
17. Maurya
18. Qutbuddin Aibak
19. Hawa Mahal
20. Jawaharlal Nehru
21. Swami Vivekananda
22. Abul Kalam Azad
23. Five
24. Nur Jahan
25. Qutb Minar

HUMAN BODY

1. Liver
2. AB negative
3. Eye
4. Hiccup
5. Edward Jenner
6. Tooth decay
7. Hands and feet
8. Small intestine
9. Ear
10. Common cold. Most adults have at least two to three colds each year, while children have as many as six to eight.

11. Skin
12. Iris
13. Ear
14. Legs
15. Twenty-four
16. Diabetes
17. Tongue
18. Liver
19. Eyelids
20. Small intestine
21. Kidney diseases
22. Kidney
23. J
24. Dentist
25. Blood

MATHS-III

1.	72	Minus	46	Multiply	4	Divide	8	=	13
2.	8	Multiply	12	Minus	26	Divide	14	=	5
3.	21	Divide	3	Plus	24	Minus	12	=	19
4.	23	Multiply	8	Minus	74	Divide	11	=	10
5.	46	Minus	24	Multiply	3	Plus	5	=	71
6.	84	Minus	47	Plus	7	Divide	22	=	2
7.	43	Plus	10	Minus	19	Divide	2	=	17
8.	25	Multiply	3	Plus	14	Minus	54	=	35

NATURE AND WILDLIFE

1. Cicada
2. Penguin. Gentoo penguins are the fastest underwater swimming birds and can reach speeds of twenty-two miles an hour.

3. It is the smallest squirrel
4. Sangai
5. Irish Wolfhound. It is the tallest of all dogs.
6. Sunderbans
7. Sikkim
8. Cattle
9. Pashmina
10. Ostrich
11. Giant panda
12. W-shaped pupils
13. *Born Free*
14. Kangaroo
15. Indonesia
16. Deer
17. German Shepherds
18. Cows
19. Blue
20. Komodo dragon
21. Jim Corbett National Park
22. Head
23. Jellyfish
24. Inside of the mouth
25. Iceland

POLITICS

1. Sri Lanka
2. Manmohan Singh
3. Dr S. Radhakrishnan
4. Jawaharlal Nehru. Jawaharlal Nehru-75 years, Indira Gandhi-67 years, Rajiv Gandhi-47 years, Sanjay Gandhi-34 years.

5. Jai Vigyan
6. V.P. Singh
7. Zail Singh
8. Sheila Dikshit
9. Two. George Washington and John Adams.
10. Presidents of India
11. K.R. Narayanan
12. Viceroy
13. Winston Churchill
14. A.P.J. Abdul Kalam
15. Lal Bahadur Shastri
16. Rajiv Gandhi
17. Jawaharlal Nehru
18. Theodore Roosevelt
19. V.P. Singh
20. J. Jayalalithaa
21. Richard Nixon
22. Pratibha Patil
23. 30 years
24. Vice-president
25. Barack Obama
26. Lakshadweep

SCIENCE AND TECHNOLOGY

1. Imagination
2. Venus
3. Larry
4. World Wide Web
5. EUROPE
6. Neptune
7. Francium

8. Afghanistan
9. Methane
10. Pumping water
11. Camera
12. Kalpana Chawla
13. Pratibha Patil
14. Land covered with snow
15. Space bar
16. Saturn
17. Glass bottle
18. Blue ticks
19. Candela; Candela, unit of luminous intensity, from candle; Hertz, unit of frequency, from the name H.R. Hertz; Pascal, unit of pressure, after Blaise Pascal; Watt, unit of power, after James Watt.
20. F1
21. Ayurveda
22. Chlorine
23. Pac-Man. Creator Toru Iwatani based it on a pizza with a slice missing.
24. Retweet
25. Isaac Newton

SPORTS-1

1. Change of decision
2. Yellow
3. Greece
4. M.S. Dhoni. Mohammad Azharuddin-174 matches, Ganguly-147 matches, M.S. Dhoni-199 matches.
5. Virat Kohli. He has scored more than 1,657 runs. After him is Rohit Sharma.

6. Sunil Gavaskar
7. Cannot be ruled offside
8. Shane Warne. Shane Warne has played 168 matches, followed by Muralitharan with 133, and Anil Kumble and Walsh with 132 each.
9. US Open
10. Buddh International Circuit
11. Sachin Tendulkar
12. Virender Sehwag
13. England
14. M.S. Dhoni
15. Mahesh Bhupathi & Leander Paes
16. Kapil Dev
17. New Zealand
18. Narain Karthikeyan
19. Judo
20. When a batsman is out on the first ball he faces
21. Beijing
22. Yuvraj Singh
23. Virat Kohli
24. Kerala
25. Gautam Gambhir

MATHS-IV

1.	19	Multiply	5	Minus	14	Divide	9	= 9
2.	18	Divide	9	Multiply	26	Minus	25	= 27
3.	13	Multiply	5	Minus	41	Divide	3	= 8
4.	38	Minus	12	Plus	34	Divide	4	= 15
5.	9	Multiply	7	Minus	5	Plus	12	= 70
6.	42	Plus	7	Divide	7	Multiply	14	= 98

| 7. | 26 | Minus | 18 | Multiply | 3 | Plus | 35 | = | 59 |
| 8. | 56 | Plus | 14 | Minus | 25 | Divide | 9 | = | 5 |

SPORTS-II

1. Cricket
2. Score a goal
3. Sachin Tendulkar
4. Lionel Messi
5. Sourav Ganguly
6. Three-banned armadillo
7. Gagan Narang
8. Manchester United
9. Sania Mirza
10. Ricky Ponting
11. Twice
12. India
13. 16
14. Polo
15. Sky blue
16. Yellow and red cards
17. Boxing
18. Athletics
19. Li Na
20. Badminton
21. Hyderabad
22. Archery
23. USA
24. Ravichandran Ashwin
25. Sachin Tendulkar (seven centuries)

TRAVEL

1. Malgudi Express
2. Panaji
3. Odisha (It is in Bhubaneswar)
4. Fatehpur Sikri
5. Rajasthan
6. Sathya Sai Baba
7. Udaipur
8. Nepal
9. Charminar
10. Kanyakumari
11. Ahmedabad
12. Nagaland
13. B.R. Ambedkar
14. Aeroplane
15. Maharashtra
16. AC Chair Car
17. Himachal Pradesh
18. Duronto
19. Sleeper
20. Amritsar
21. Maharashtra
22. Lucknow
23. None
24. Rivers
25. Mother Teresa

BUZZER ROUND-ANSWERS

SET-1

1. 1,050 gm of cotton

2. Rajendra Prasad
3. Mount Fuji
4. Leopard. It means people can't change their basic nature.
5. Valentina Tereshkova
6. Brain
7. Serious
8. Kai Po Che. It is based on the novel *The Three Mistakes of My Life* by Chetan Bhagat.
9. Tamil Nadu
10. Mumbai

SET-2

1. Polio
2. Nepal
3. Barack Obama
4. Pandit Ravi Shankar
5. Serious
6. Hong Kong
7. Kasuti
8. Walt Disney, about Mickey Mouse
9. Yellow
10. Grand Trunk Road

SET-3

1. Albert Einstein
2. Winston Churchill
3. Shri
4. January
5. Sanskrit
6. Polar bears

7. Tamil Nadu
8. Salman Khan
9. Gateway of India
10. Dhyan Chand

SET-4

1. Afghanistan
2. Mouth
3. Sachin Tendulkar
4. Serious
5. Kareena Kapoor
6. Republic Day
7. Fourteen
8. Queen Victoria
9. A.P.J. Abdul Kalam
10. Control

SET-5

1. Kohinoor diamond
2. Neon
3. Japan
4. Ben 10
5. Gujarat; in the Gir Forest.
6. Swan
7. Ganesha. Celebrations for Ganesh Chaturthi usually fall between 20 August and 15 September every year.
8. Rickshaw
9. Norah Jones
10. Six. Blue, yellow, black, green, red and white.

SET-6

1. Bahadur Shah Zafar
2. Protein; from proteios.
3. June
4. Hair
5. Chhota Bheem
6. Rupee sign
7. Munshi Premchand
8. Earthquakes
9. Joking. He is a golf player.
10. Tansen

SET-7

1. Napoleon
2. Monitor
3. Bangladesh
4. Red panda
5. Odisha
6. Polonius
7. Antarctica
8. Stumps
9. Moon; from luna; from the belief that changes in the moon caused intermittent insanity.
10. Subscriber

SET-8

1. Nectar
2. Odisha
3. Platinum
4. Cricket; from criquer.
5. Jaggu

6. White
7. *Alice's Adventures in Wonderland*
8. Satpura Range
9. Rahul Dravid
10. Bold

SET-9

1. Mughal
2. Paper
3. Oxygen
4. Kangaroo
5. Rocket
6. Cancellation
7. Charles Dickens
8. Ganga
9. Saina Nehwal
10. Indigo

SET-10

1. Amjad Ali Khan
2. Joking. It has been shared on four occasions.
3. Rajasthan
4. Neon; from neos.
5. Polar bear
6. White
7. Shah Rukh Khan
8. Lemuel Gulliver
9. 20-20
10. Venezuela

SET-11

1. Pandit Ravi Shankar
2. Stamp
3. Fatehpur Sikri
4. Saturn
5. Alexander Graham Bell
6. Bharat Ratna
7. Serious
8. Captain America
9. Hindi
10. P.T. Usha

SET-12

1. Jammu
2. Red
3. Interpol (from Inter[national] pol[ice])
4. Elephanta Caves
5. Train
6. Akhilesh Yadav
7. Sambar
8. Joking. It starts in April.
9. William Shakespeare
10. Goose

SET-13

1. Gum
2. Taj Mahal
3. Neil Armstrong
4. Chhota Bheem
5. Tiger
6. Yoga

7. Shatranj or chess. The story was 'Shatranj Ke Khiladi' and was also made into a film by Satyajit Ray.
8. Sachin Tendulkar
9. Serious
10. Bullseye

SET-14

1. Nobel Prize
2. Maharashtra
3. Rubber
4. Sahadeva
5. Uttar Pradesh
6. Joking. Both the male and female have tusks.
7. Pumpkin
8. Serious
9. Lakshadweep
10. Red

SET-15

1. Maurya
2. Akshay Kumar
3. Joking. It is named after the Greek word for the 'sun'.
4. Holi
5. Lion
6. Oliver Twist
7. Brahmaputra
8. Cricket
9. The Philippines
10. Lord Krishna

SET-16

1. Investigation
2. The Great Wall of China
3. Dadasaheb Phalke Award
4. Serious
5. 36 (Chattees), Chhattisgarh
6. Joking. Around 40 per cent of Brazil's total area comprises of the Amazon Rainforest.
7. Mongoose
8. Football
9. Mulberry
10. Queen Victoria

SET-17

1. Tram
2. Panipat
3. Batman/Bruce Wayne
4. Marie Curie
5. Serious
6. Phalguna. It corresponds with February-March in the Gregorian calendar.
7. Gulliver himself
8. Africa
9. Anil Kumble
10. Joking; clams and mussels can also produce pearls.

SET-18

1. Silk
2. Freedom
3. C.V. Raman
4. Uncle

5. Literature
6. Olive Ridley turtles. They come to nest on the Odisha coast.
7. Mowgli
8. Kings XI Punjab
9. Serious
10. Ton

SET-19

1. A
2. Sanchi
3. Lunch box
4. Janmashtami
5. Joking. Almost 97 per cent of an orangutan's genetic makeup is the same as a human's.
6. *Panchatantra*
7. Mountain
8. Australia
9. Thousand
10. Neptune

SET-20

1. Seven
2. Shivaji
3. Jaya Bhaduri/Jaya Bachchan
4. First X-ray. Rtntgen's first X-ray photographs of his wife Anna Bertha's hand, with the bones and a ring on her third finger clearly visible, had a profound effect worldwide.
5. Joking. The koala is a marsupial.
6. Saffron

7. Meghaduta
8. Jammu
9. Dhyan Chand
10. Red

SET-21

1. None. 10 lakh = 1 million.
2. Harshavardhana
3. Chacha Chaudhary
4. River Dolphin
5. Moon
6. *Hamlet*
7. Lakshadweep
8. M.S. Dhoni
9. Cube
10. Serious

SET-22

1. Mother
2. Qutb Minar. 379 steps.
3. Barack Obama
4. Republic Day
5. Joking. A guinea pig is a rodent.
6. Six
7. Macbeth
8. West Bengal; Darjeeling Zoo.
9. Karate
10. Towel

SET-23

1. Kerala

2. Woman
3. Joking
4. Boa constrictor
5. Xylophone
6. Hanuman
7. Spider
8. Madhya Pradesh
9. Four
10. Joking

SET-24

1. Regional; South Asian Association for Regional Cooperation.
2. Buddha
3. Calcium
4. Serious
5. Jagjit Singh
6. Kerala
7. David Copperfield
8. Antarctica
9. French Open
10. China

SET-25

1. Mount Everest
2. Humayun
3. Marie Curie
4. Serious
5. Amjad Khan
6. Haryana
7. Wolf

8. Mizoram
9. Hairstyles
10. Horse

www.ingramcontent.com/pod-product-compliance
Lightning Source LLC
Chambersburg PA
CBHW032050150426
43194CB00006B/476